ENGINES

of

WEALTH

COMMERCIAL
RETAIL SHOPS

PHILLIP KING
STEPHEN HAINS

Engines of Wealth - Commercial Retail Shops © Phillip King 2018
Co-author Stephen Hains

ISBN: 978-1-925732-54-2 (paperback)

Disclaimer
The following content, strategies and practical examples have been developed by the author Phillip King over many years of investing in both residential and commercial retail property. The author would like to point out that he is not a financial planner nor is he offering financial advice. The contents of this book is simply an insight into the way Phillip was able to build wealth through investing in Commercial Retail Shops and provides the reader background on the strategies he deployed.

It should be noted that past performance does not guarantee future performance and the examples provided are for general information only. Before making any investment decision readers should always seek the advice of a licenced financial planner who will take into account your personal investment objectives, financial situation and individual needs.

If you have any questions or are seeking general information pertaining to the contents of this book please go to the website www.EnginesofWealth.com.

Cataloguing-in-Publication information for this title is listed with the National Library of Australia.

Published in Australia by Phillip King and InHouse Publishing.

www.enginesofwealth.com
www.inhousepublishing.com.au

CONTENTS

PREFACE

The world of finance and investment choices is daunting. In fact, many of us shy away from it, never seeking guidance to navigate our way. This book serves to explain the mystery of retail property investment. It is useful for all ages, from teenage children through to elderly parents. *Engines of Wealth* will explain how to create financial wealth that will stand the test of time.

I am confident the guidance provided here will help those of any generation secure their financial freedom, not because I have university degrees stating that I am a financial guru, but because I have almost 30 years' experience in investment wins and losses. I have fine-tuned my strategy with expert advice, trying many approaches. Ultimately, I have found that retail property investment is the best asset source for building wealth — wealth that will extend well beyond my approaching retirement. My passion for wealth creation and building a secure future income gives me confidence that the lessons I have learned in securing success can serve as a valuable resource for others.

So, where does the journey begin? We become conscious of our desire to be free of the grinding concerns of money at different ages. For some, this occurs in primary school. For others it is a teenage awakening. For those lucky enough to make it into the workforce before thinking about money, there is nothing like a 60-hour-week at the hands of an inconsiderate boss to spark dreams of financial freedom.

You may think that to be financially free you need millions of dollars. In reality, the dream of living comfortably can be readily achieved through planning, time, and an investment portfolio that generates a steady income. Instead of looking for a winning lottery ticket, a steady income of $100,000 per year indexed to inflation may be all you need to live your financial freedom dream.

You may often ask yourself, "What could I do to get rich?" or "How can I make more money?" or "What should I invest in to become a millionaire?" Our parents often told us to knuckle down, work harder, do more overtime, and save our money. Of course, as your experience grows and the value you offer to your company increases, over time you can seek out higher pay and better jobs. But, "What should you do with this extra money?" That is the real question. Will you increase your savings, or simply afford a more comfortable lifestyle? Invariably, these approaches may increase your financial savings, allowing you and your family to have possessions, but for 98% of us this rarely results in creating real wealth.

I think one of the best books I have read on dispelling the myth that only the highly-educated and career-minded end up wealthy, was Rich Dad, Poor Dad by Robert Kiyosaki. Kiyosaki's book explains that building wealth requires a level of entrepreneurialism and risk, pursuing an investment model that can be scaled and is rarely achieved by simply securing a highly paid job and a focus on saving.

I believe the foundation for creating a long-lasting income stream is leverage. The age-old proverb "you need to borrow money to make money" rings true. Unless you receive a large inheritance, you alone will be responsible for etching out your position in life; you alone will need to create your wealth. The first myth we must dispel is that you need to amass a large fortune in the bank. I live with a large amount of debt. However, that debt secures positively geared property that generates a monthly income, which I can comfortably live on for the rest of my life. Better still, it will be there for many years after my death to fuel the fortunes of my children.

The problem many people face is that their extra effort and overtime does not result in long-lasting riches because they do not invest it. I once heard a statement that I like to quote:

> "You don't have to be rich to invest, but you have to
> invest to be rich." [1]

Of course, many people roll their eyes at me in despair, believing that they need a better job with a bigger salary to become an investor. What they must understand is the power of time, which influences even small amounts of invested money, to develop significant wealth. All too often, younger people decide that investing is something they'll do down the track when they can afford it. Life goes on and, guess what? Those kids turn into adults. Many are still waiting for their next pay rise, so that they can start investing. It is this attitude that I am re-programming in my kids. Investing a small percentage of your weekly income from early on in life ensures that it becomes part of a lifelong routine.

So, the $64 question is "How do we get rich?" When I discuss this question with work colleagues, especially those fresh out of university with the world at their feet, I ask them:

> "Who would you ask for advice if you wanted to
> become rich?"

[1] Warren Buffet, CEO Berkshire Hathaway

The top three answers I regularly receive are these:

1) I'd ask a Financial Planner

My daughter often says to me, "Dad, no offence, but–" right before she offends me!

I often find myself in the same position. Here goes: No offence to the financial planning industry, but I have found the top priority of financial planners is to sell you insurance. Their focus is ensuring that you have the right life insurance policies in place. The three key policies they will propose tend to be Life Insurance, Total and Permanent Disability Insurance, and Income Protection insurance.

Their sales pitch is extremely compelling, "If you get injured out there and can't work, who is going to look after the kids? Pay the bills? What about the mortgage? And your medical expenses? Will you be able to keep a roof over your head?" Very compelling stuff. Just to be clear, I think we all should have these insurance policies to protect ourselves and our family. The area where many get it wrong, however, is that they spend too much for a suitable amount of cover. When we are in our 20s our payout cover needs to be higher than when we are in our 50s — not just because we have longer to live at 20, but because when we are 50 we will, hopefully, have assets that can support us. This means that, at 50, you don't need as much cover to provide a comfortable living. The common trap many fall into is that they don't revisit their level of cover and they miss the opportunity to lower their insurance premiums.

Life insurance premiums are a lucrative business for financial planners because the Trailing Edge commissions are typically paid out monthly for the life of the insurance policy, and this can often span several decades.

The business of securing insurance is very different from the business of designing a wealth-building strategy. Your challenge, therefore, is to find a financial planner who will recommend a wealth-building strategy, as opposed to an insurance portfolio. They should be advising you on how to establish a long-term investment roadmap, and the right investment vehicles to optimise the journey, such as trust funds and company structures, right through to managing your superannuation.

I remember one financial planner turning up to my house in quite a beaten-up Hyundai. I thought to myself, Is this the guy I want giving me financial advice? Ah, no! Sure enough, after I told him my life insurance policies were all in place through my super-annuation fund and I wasn't interested in revisiting those, he had very little to discuss.

Over the years, I have accepted free Financial Planning Sessions offered by banks. I have sat through many sessions and, invariably, it has been difficult to get them away from wanting to position life insurance. For me, the jury is out on them and whether they help you create a long-lasting plan to achieve real wealth. I guess my bias toward property provides little incentive for financial planners, hence our wealth strategies follow different paths.

2) I'd ask my Accountant

My uncle is an accountant and this answer does indeed resonate with me as I have learned a lot from Uncle John. The world of investing is closely tied to the world of taxation: to be a good investor, tax considerations are paramount, and who better to understand taxation than an accountant. Accountants are certainly exposed to many different types of investors and, of course, they regularly prepare tax returns for high net-worth individuals, claiming lucrative tax deductions across many investment types.

I think leveraging the skills of an accountant to seek out wealth-building ideas is a great place to start. However, I also believe it is somewhat hit and miss. In my case, Uncle John was an accountant second. His real passion was property investment and property development. So, I was extremely fortunate to have had him in my life. I used him as a sounding board on every investment decision I made — he encouraged me, inspired me and ultimately guided me along the path I chose to build wealth.

Other accountants may not be as passionate about investing and may lack the key knowledge that certifies them as an expert on how to build wealth — that is having wealth themselves. In the real world, most accountants simply keep score; you tell them what you earned last year, and they tell you how much tax you need to pay. Basically, accountants ensure that you are claiming all allowable deductions, and that your business is set up to legally minimise tax obligations.

I have used the same accountant for many years, seeing him once a year to do my tax return. From time to time, I may call him to question if an expense is of a capital or operational nature, on which he provides sound advice. However, in all of our years, whenever I have asked "Hey Ian, what's your recommendation on building wealth?", he has always replied, "You're doing well enough, stick to what you know."

3) I'd ask a lawyer

Lawyers are a valuable resource along the road to riches. However, they are guided by law, not an individual's financial gain. They work in six-minute charging increments, and are not educated in long-term planning or financial strategy.

So, a lawyer is not the answer to the financial dream. But they are a great ally to ensure that whatever wealth-building strategy you use is within the law and operated legally.

Back to my question, "Who do I ask if I want to build wealth?" Occasionally, I get an answer that hits the nail on the head:

"You ask the richest person you know!"

Knowledge is certainly king in building wealth, and there are many ways to make money. If you are fortunate enough to know someone who has built great wealth, ask them to share how they did it. Most successful people don't mind sharing their knowledge and helping others. For some there's that element of bragging. Whatever way it is offered, all advice is valuable.

In most wealth-building books, there is the comment: "Congratulations! By picking up this book you have taken the first step towards improving your financial outlook". This makes you feel that real wealth is just around the corner and pats you on the back for seeking out more knowledge.

I felt it was important to start my book with this conversation, as there are many ways to make money and build wealth. Each year, I buy a copy of the BRW Rich 200 List and enjoy reading about the many types of millionaires, and the various ways they created their wealth. Some make it big in business, others in fashion, soft drinks, chocolate, and, while property has a big following, in general, if you name an industry, I bet someone has made a million dollars from it.

For those who don't have a multi-millionaire to mentor you, or if you are uncomfortable talking about money, then this book shares my passion and wisdom. What will you learn? What knowledge can I pass on to you? Well, it is simply the way I have personally built long-lasting wealth. It is the way that worked for me, but by no means is it the only way.

I have built long-lasting wealth through investing in positively geared retail commercial property, i.e. the buildings that house cafés, hairdressers, restaurants, bakeries, and doctors' surgeries. These properties produce a secure income stream that is indexed to inflation and tax effective, and one that will last well beyond my expiry date.

Chapter 1

YOUR INVESTMENT CHOICES

Now that you have committed to begin the journey of building wealth and you recognise that it will not happen overnight, there is one principle that is fundamental: we must invest to be rich. I was 24 when I put my wealth engine into first gear. The fuel in the tank was leverage. The principle I have applied since the beginning is that, if I can leverage more money, I can invest in more assets to build wealth.

The warning here is that, when your engine moves into 4th gear, while it means that you are leveraged and successfully building wealth, you are also likely to owe the bank between $1 million and $10 million. Some people cannot sleep at night knowing that they owe this much, even if their assets are securing the debt. If your tolerance for debt, and hence leverage, is low then your wealth engine will take longer to reach top speed. You may find, as I did, that as you move through the gears and understand how leverage works in your favour, your appetite for debt — and hence your speed for building wealth will increase. I am in the 5th gear of my wealth engine, and I have always slept well.

Let me demonstrate what I mean with an example. If I had $20,000 to invest and received a healthy return of 10%, in this day of volatile share markets and economies, I would be over the moon. I would make a profit of $2,000. However, if I invested $1,000,000 in a safe asset class at a conservative 5% return then I would make a profit of $50,000. This example demonstrates that building wealth becomes easier if larger sums of money are available. For me, and my sound sleep, I look to invest in an asset class that has security and one against which banks readily lend large sums of money.

My wealth journey began small, but I was always thinking big. As this book's title indicates, my preferred asset investment class is retail property. I learned quickly that this investment type drives long-term, secure wealth. However, you can consider several other investment options, especially when in first gear and looking to build the base equity for investment. Many financial planners will advise you (once they have moved on from insurance) to have a diverse financial portfolio. However, diversity does not always mean security, nor does it mean that your portfolio gets the best return. You are right to ask that critical question,

What investment options are available today?

To many, the options appear vast and confusing. Let's simplify them, discussing the pros and cons. In my opinion, there are only three places to invest money **cash, shares, and property.** All other investment options are derived from these three. You may have heard of many other options, but let's investigate how many come under my three, core investment categories:

CASH	SHARES	PROPERTY
Fixed Interest Deposits	Australian Stock Exchange	Residential Houses
Government Bonds	Global Stock Markets	Residential Units
Short-Term Lending	Futures	Retail Commercial Shops
	Options	Commercial Offices
	Share Market Indices	Commercial Factories
	Precious Metal Stocks	Rural Farms
	CFD Trading	Vacant Land
	Industry Funds	Development Land

By dividing all choices into these three investment categories, you can more easily review their strengths, drawbacks, and suitability as your wealth-building engine. Firstly, let's look at:

CASH

I am one of the first to admit that cash is king, but cash deposited in the bank has one main enemy, inflation. Inflation devalues your money over time. A good example is when you look at what things cost today compared with what they cost ten years ago. A can of coke purchased a decade ago cost $1; today it costs around $3. So, over time, your money does not buy the same amount of goods it once did. A measure of inflation is tracked and published annually by every country's government. In Australia, this is called the Consumer Price Index or CPI.

Typically, Australia's CPI can run anywhere from 1–3% in a given year. So, when banks are only offering you 2.5% p.a. interest on your deposits, after adjusting for inflation, your return is less than 1%. And don't forget taxation, which also erodes the interest benefit, depending on your tax bracket. The bottom line is that if you leave your investment funds in the bank, its buying power will lose value over time.

When you set out on your journey towards building wealth the first hurdle, whether you are young or old, is the initial investment deposit. At least, with cash, this is not a problem. You can deposit as little as $1 or $1,000 in the bank and begin enjoying the power of compound interest over time. Couple this with a weekly savings plan, and you're on your way to growth, albeit slowly. I also hear you saying, "Have you seen the interest rates the banks are offering today?", and I agree that with rates sub 2.5% you'll need to live to be 100 before making it rich. For those of you who are impatient to achieve wealth, you need to consider another option.

There is one more problem I have with cash as a wealth-building vehicle. To build real wealth through an investment strategy in one life-time, you need one powerful tool and that is:

Leverage.

To create real wealth, you must be able to borrow money. You don't want to be making 10% on $100,000; you want to make 10% on $1,000,000, so your investment vehicle needs to provide you with the capacity to borrow money from the bank. Can you do that with cash? No! It is not possible to borrow money from the bank to invest in fixed-term cash deposits — banks will always charge you more interest to borrow than they will pay for your deposits. If you are retired and have no appetite for leverage and risk then cash is king, but, as an investment vehicle, be it bonds or fixed interest deposits, cash is out.

Let's take a look at your second investment category:

SHARES

The stock market as a platform for wealth-building is well known to many, yet mastered by few. Stories of great success are tempered by those of enormous loss. Those who win are either very smart, very well resourced, or very lucky. I come from the school of hard knocks and, although I like to buy the odd lottery ticket, I prefer investments to be within my control and not affected by the daily mood swings of the stock market.

The stock market has always attracted me. Tales of amazing gains made in weeks or days instead of years were too tempting to resist. The thought of owning a share in some of the world's most successful companies, like Apple, IBM, Coke-a-Cola, BHP, or AT&T, and sharing in their profits and growth is reassuring. On the surface, this appears as an exceptional wealth-creation vehicle. However, it is also littered with nightmares of spectacular market collapses and companies that have gone broke, including HIH and Bearings Bank. In many cases, corruption or mismanagement led to the demise of these once great, global companies. In each case, shareholder value was wiped out along with the livelihoods and dreams of countless individuals.

For me, the stock market is a great place to build a deposit when beginning the wealth journey. However, once you have reached your deposit goals, enabling you to buy a property, I suggest you get your money out. While your money is on the stock market, several techniques can minimise your risk of loss, and reduce the fees you pay to expensive brokers. Consider investing in managed funds that trade a portfolio of stocks, including local, international, fixed and indexed. The Australian Financial Investment Corporation (AFI) is a fund that simply buys shares in the top 200 Australian companies each year. By definition, they are diversified across industries (but not globally) and they don't use expensive analysts to pick stocks, so their fees are lower.

I like shares to build a deposit, but I don't like shares as a wealth-building engine, and that comes back to leverage. You need an investment vehicle that enables you to borrow lots of money safely and, unfortunately, there is nothing safe about a market that is re-valued every minute of every hour of every day. If sentiment on the market is negative, your stock value could take a downturn for no apparent reason. Swings of 10–20 percent occur regularly, i.e. once or twice a decade. The problem for investors is that banks like to ensure that their Loan to Value Ratio (or LVR) stays within their lending policies. So, you may get what is called a Margin Call, asking you to chip in that 10–20% of equity you just lost. We look deeper into LVRs in the next chapter.

In your early years, when your share portfolio is small, you may recover that lost 10–20% in a few months. But later, when your portfolio is significant, maybe even in the millions, the odds of you having that 20% on hand to cover a margin call may be slim. If you don't have the money to top up your LVR, banks will sell your portfolio and take their money back. This instantly crystallises your loss and leaves you out of pocket. For that reason, shares are ruled out as part of my wealth-building engine — you just wouldn't be able to sleep at night.

We have now ruled out two of the three investment categories we are reviewing for long-term investment of our money. This leaves us with only one:

PROPERTY

Firstly, there are many different property types that you can consider for an investment vehicle:

- Residential, including houses, units, apartments, town houses
- Commercial, including offices, retail shops, warehouses, factories
- Rural, including farms and ranches
- Vacant land, for use to build any of the above

When looking at each property type, you need to do so while considering your primary investment objectives:

1) To create wealth that stands the test of time
2) To create an income stream, indexed to inflation, that will free you from your day job
3) To provide a tax-effective investment structure

Putting aside my own philosophical issues with cash and shares, historically, they have not helped investors achieve the above long-term objectives.

With these three investment mantras in mind, you can quickly eliminate vacant land and rural properties as investment vehicles. Land on its own does not offer an income stream, rural farms can be difficult to let, and seasonality makes farms a feast or a famine. The primary drawback for rural farms is the specific farming skills and background required to operate such businesses, not to mention the risk of bad weather that results in an unreliable income source. For me, these property types do not provide the secure, reliable, consistent income at the core of a wealth-building plan.

Although a block of land is not my preferred source of wealth-building, I do recognise the importance of this asset class and accept it is the foundation of other property types. Without land, we have nothing to build our lives upon. The value of land and its con-tribution to wealth is well captured in one of my favourite poems, entitled *WHO AM I?* Written by an unknown author.

WHO AM I?

I am the basis of all wealth, the heritage of the wise, the thrifty, and the prudent.

I am the poor man's joy and comfort, the rich man's prize, the right hand of capital, the silent partner of many thousands of successful men.

I am the solace of the widow, the comfort of old age, the cornerstone of security against misfortune and want.

I am handed down to children through generations as a thing of great worth. I am the choicest fruit of toil, credit respects me. Yet I am humble. I stand before every man bidding him to know me for what I am, and possess me.

I grow and increase in value through countless days. Though I seem dormant, my worth increases, never failing, never ceasing. Time is my aid and population heaps upon my gain. Fire and the elements I defy, for they cannot destroy me.

My possessors learn to believe in me, invariably they become envied. While all things wither and decay, I survive. The centuries find me younger, increasing in my strength.

I am the foundation of banks, the producer of food, and the basis of all wealth throughout the world. Yet I am so common that thousands, unthinking and unknowing, pass me by.

I AM LAND!

Commercial and Residential Property

Let's turn our attention to commercial and residential properties. Commercial properties include retail shops, offices, warehouses and factories. Owning a small factory or warehouse has always interested me and, over the past decade, I have seen excellent gains in this asset class. The challenge, however, is the large number of owner occupiers in this asset class: factory tenants like to own their own premises as it not only secures their family's future; they are often located near the area they service or close to the family home, reducing their commute time.

This high rate of owner-occupiers reduces not only the supply of quality factories and warehouses, but also the number of available tenants. The result is greater risk on rental returns should the tenant depart, resulting in a potentially lengthy vacancy period while you find an adequate replacement. Due to this volatility, and the constrained supply/demand pool, I choose to avoid this asset class. I guess I prefer to swim in a deeper pool.

Office space is an asset class in which I have some investment experience, but this was only a consequence of purchasing a retail shop that came with an office. I have never sort to procure office space investments on their own, but I have inherited offices into my portfolio as they are often located above retail shops and come as a package deal.

As the local and global economies have slowed and we have experienced modest economic growth, office space rents have stagnated, providing an ample supply. At the time of writing this book, I have two small offices that have been vacant for over 18 months. Given the difficulties in securing tenants and oversupply in most capital cities today, an oversupply that has not changed in the past 10 years, I recommend discounting offices as your wealth-building vehicle.

After working through the pros and cons of several property assets, you are left with two remaining property types as the fuel for your wealth engine:

1) Residential property
2) Commercial retail shops

Residential Property

Residential property is the preferred investment asset class for most property investors. I once read that there are 40 times more residential investors in the market than commercial investors.

My view is that your domestic residence should form the foundation of your property portfolio. After all, the great "Australian Dream" is to own your own home and watch the kids grow up in the backyard. The federal government even provides us a major incentive to ensure we all pursue this dream. Your home is the one real tax haven today that allows you to build wealth without accruing any tax liability. That is why I encourage you to buy a domicile residence as the first property in your portfolio. It is your first step on your way to wealth.

The long-running debate in economics of "buying vs renting" persists as the ebb and flow of interest rates makes one more attractive than the other. I have a long-term, pragmatic view. If leverage is the fuel for your wealth engine, you cannot build leverage when you are renting, only when you are owning.

I suggest that you buy a house or unit and move into it as soon as you save a deposit. It then becomes and remains your domicile residence for six years, even if you move back in with mum and dad and decide to rent it out. Your domicile residence will start to grow in value and build in equity — equity that provides leverage for your investment strategy for many years to come. This equity is exempt from any government tax when you sell or upgrade, provided the home has remained your domicile residence.

Residential property, like all other asset classes, is not immune from market downturns. So, to maximise the equity growth, you need to avoid buying property in the peak of an overvalued residential market. Unfortunately, today most residential markets in Australia are trading at the top of the market, so I recommend that you do your research. Try to buy properties that are at the entry level of the market, for example units and small houses in growing suburbs. This ensures that demand remains strong for the property. As you enter at the bottom of the property market today to get a foothold, in a few years, when you want to leverage the equity in this property, other first-time buyers will be looking to enter this end of the market.

The final remaining property asset class is:

Commercial Retail Property

Commercial retail property is an asset class you walk past everyday of your life. You typically patronise these establishments without knowing their worth or contemplating owning them. We are talking about investing in the buildings that house the retail businesses that provide you with essential services. Hairdressers, doctors, vets, accountants, lawyers, restaurants, supermarkets, bottle shops, takeaways, chemists, newsagents, beauticians, bakeries, optometrists and real estate agents are all examples of commercial retail property tenants. Remember, you are interested in owning the buildings, not the businesses themselves. Your tenants are the proprietors of these businesses.

What I like about commercial retail property is the way these premises are traded. The valuation method and purchasing process is based on a mathematical formula designed to deliver the investor a positive income stream or investment return, i.e. take the shop's annual net rent, divide this by the return you are seeking, and this results in the price you pay for the building. This takes much of the emotion out of the pursuit, unlike a residential property where prices are often driven up by an emotional connection to the property, such as being near a beach, a school, the shopping mall or public transport.

Residential property is purchased very differently from commercial property. Around 70% of the residential property market is owner-occupied where the price for this property class is typically based on feelings. Residential properties are frequently purchased without regard for their financial return. Many owners are not concerned about making an annual profit — it's the lifestyle they are investing in, not the annual return. It is for this reason that most residential properties are purchased at prices that leave an investor negatively-geared. What that means is the ongoing expenses and bank interest incurred each year is more than the rent the property would generate if rented to a tenant, resulting in an annual investment loss.

Commercial retail property, on the other hand, is valued and purchased according to a formula that is designed to provide the investor with a positively geared return. Making a profit in residential property relies on the property increasing in value each year to deliver the investor a profit above the property's annual holding costs, which produce a negative income. Buying a retail commercial property delivers the investor a positive income stream that provides a solid cashflow, not only this year, but for many years to come, and it is indexed to inflation, with annual rental increases built into the lease. It is these annual rental increases that ensure capital growth for the investor because the building's valuation method is tied to the rent.

In later chapters, I will demonstrate how building wealth requires you to procure multiple properties, thereby requiring you to invest in an asset class that allows you to scale your portfolio. To do this, you need assets that produce positive cashflow rather than negative cashflow. Otherwise, the banks will put the brakes on your wealth-building aspirations. Walking into a bank manager when you own a cashflow-positive property and asking for more money is much easier than walking in with a negatively-geared property that is tying up your cash.

The security of your weekly cashflow is of paramount concern to your bank manager. For residential property investments, the leases you enter into with tenants are typically 6–12 month terms. This offers the bank little security over future mortgage repayments, and poor visibility into the tenant's long-term commitment. Leases for commercial property, however, are typically three, five, or up to ten years in length, and are secured by the tenant's residential property. This offers the bank excellent security over future mortgage repayments.

A supermarket chain once signed a 15-year lease with me with two, five-year options. They clearly wanted to protect their fit-out investment and planned to operate there for 25 years. Of course, the banks loved the extra security, but the other bonus was that property buyers also valued more highly this property with its long lease and secure tenant. The value of my building went up just by signing a longer lease.

Residential tenants are generally more transient than commercial tenants — they move around more often, depending on their circumstances and personal relationships. Conversely, retail shop tenants, whose income and job security is tied to the property, tend to remain. Banks place a high importance on this dependence on the lease. Put simply, retail shop tenants are stickier than residential tenants. Each time a tenant moves on, you are likely to suffer a short vacancy period and financial loss, but this occurs more regularly with residential tenants.

Continuity in tenancy is why retail commercial leases tend to be signed for terms of three, five and even ten years. A tenant's livelihood and job security are directly related to the security they hold over the premises. The longer the lease, the more secure their business is and the higher its value to a potential buyer, if sold. For you, the landlord, this is reassuring as it means your rent and ability to meet the mortgage is guaranteed for many years to come, and the banks love that.

Over the years, my experience too is that residential tenants do not look after the place as if it was their own home. Many won't mow the lawn, maintain the gardens, or clean as often as you would like. When the property becomes rundown, they simply move out and lease a property in better condition, leaving you with the restoration bill. Invariably, as the landlord, you are left with a property to overhaul: painting, cleaning carpets, mowing lawns, cleaning kitchens, scouring or replacing ovens. I once spent over $10,000 bringing a residential property back to a reasonable letting state after a short, 12-month tenancy. The $2,000 rental bond I kept did not cover restoration costs and the chances of pursuing the tenants in court for damages was not worth my time or effort. Tenants often have little wealth or assets of any significant value that you can recover. If you were to pursue them, the only person who would get paid is your lawyer.

So, another major benefit of owning commercial retail investments over residential property is that the repairs and maintenance costs are significantly less. Firstly, most commercial retail shops consist of a concrete floor, three brick walls, and a glass shop front — not a lot can go wrong that is the responsibility of the owner. In most leases, tenants are responsible for taking out insurance cover on the glass shopfront and for maintaining the door and hinges because it is their customers coming in and out who cause wear and tear. Retail shops are a place of business and are critical to the tenant making their living, so the property's presentation is important to them and they will spend their own money to ensure that their shop is well-presented for customers to have a pleasant shopping experience.

One key differentiator of the commercial tenant is that their livelihood and wealth is tied to maintaining the lease — paying their rent and keeping the shop presentable are their top priorities. Retail tenants do not want to breach their leases as this could potentially lead to their lease being terminated and them losing their job and business asset. So, when we compare the maintenance requirements of a residential property versus retail shops, shops come out a clear winner.

A few other factors support shops over residential properties as an investment. One is in regards to your access to a guarantee, should anything go wrong. Typically, retail property tenants are home owners (not renters), and they sign personal guarantees over their lease. This, in effect, gives you their house as security over future rental payments. A residential tenant typically has no assets to serve as security if they default, other than a four-week bond.

Another factor to consider is ease of eviction, if required. In a commercial lease, you have greater rights to lock the doors and evict tenants who do not pay their rent — a stark contrast to the residential world where courts worry about vulnerable people and children being left homeless on the streets. A commercial shop is leased for the purposes of making a profit, i.e. the tenant or their children do not live or reside in the property, and therefore no one will be evicted if you lock the doors. Residential property evictions too can take several months, and require complicated legal proceedings to secure enforceable eviction orders.

The best part for you as an investor in a retail property is that the tenant is working for you, looking after your building and, in most cases, improving its value — not destroying it, as can occur in the residential world. Commercial tenants will strive to keep their shops neat and tidy with a modern, fresh appearance for their customers. I have seen many leases that contain clauses obligating a tenant to refresh their fit-out every five years, which ensures that the value of your commercial asset is maintained. The tenant's fit-out will not only improve the value of your property, it will draw in more customers, thus enhancing the value of every other business in the centre. Compare that with the residential tenant who rarely performs any maintenance, and never spends any of their own money improving the premises.

Being a financially-oriented person who wants to build wealth in a methodical manner, I find commercial shops are by far the best asset class to use as a wealth-building strategy: they provide long-term security, ease of maintenance, dependability, tenant reliability and, best of all, they are positively geared, generating you an income stream. It is this income stream that will be viewed favourably by your bank manager, enabling you to borrow more and continue to scale your portfolio.

I would like to re-state my position on residential property as a vital foundation for any investment portfolio. If you can afford to acquire a residential property to live in, doing that as your first property makes good sense. Your domicile residence is tax-free, so having this as the foundation of your portfolio is one of the most tax-effective things you can do. If you can't afford a residential property straight away, read on because, in later chapters, I will cover how to use retail property as your stepping stone to achieving residential ownership.

After securing your domicile (residential) property, I propose that you acquire retail property as the second and subsequent properties for your portfolio. These engines of wealth will deliver positive income that will further fuel your investment strategy, setting you on your road to riches.

Chapter 2

RESIDENTIAL VERSUS COMMERCIAL PROPERTY

LET'S DO THE MATHS

With the strengths and weaknesses of various investment choices revealed in Chapter 1, calculating how both residential and retail property investments build wealth over time is critical. When I started my wealth-building journey, my initial focus was residential property. By the age of 35, I had built a portfolio of five residential properties. Therefore, I am well-placed to discuss the pros and cons of each asset class. I currently have no residential assets other than my domicile residence and, together with my partners, I have a commercial portfolio of 51 shops.

The place to start is understanding why investors buy a neg-atively-geared residential property versus a positively geared commercial shop. To better explain this, I will run through a few real-world examples.

Let's start with residential property. Tom purchased a house for $600,000. After paying $23,000 in stamp duty tax to the State government and $8,000 in legal and conveyancing costs, the property cost Tom a total of $631,000. As a rental property, the annual balance sheet looked like this:

Income

Rent ($520/week)	$ 27,040.00
Expenses	
Loan Interest (5% on $631,000)	$ 31,550.00
Council Rates	$ 950.00
Water Rates	$ 870.00
Building Insurance	$ 1,200.00
Repairs and Maintenance[2]	$ 1,500.00
Total	$ 36,070.00

Negatively-geared annual loss (Income – Expenses) =   **-$ 9,030.00**

---

[2] Repairs and Maintenance is a fund for minor building upkeep, painting, electrical repairs, replacing the stove, hot water system, etc. This fund may not be used in a year, but when considering the total cost of a house maintenance is important.

If Tom had purchased the above residential property for investment purposes, he would be losing $9,030 each year, hence the term negatively-geared. Because Tom is providing much-needed accommodation to the rental market, the government allows Tom the ability to write off this loss against his taxable income, thereby providing Tom a tax refund at the end of each year. If Tom currently pays tax at a rate of 30 cents in the dollar, he receives a ($9,030 × 30%) = $2,709 tax refund for this loss, effectively minimising Tom's annual loss on the property to ($9,030 - $2,709) = $6,321 each year.

The real value in picking the right residential investment is maximising capital growth. Selecting a building and location that is growing in value, hopefully quicker than the market, is key to optimising profit. As an investor, Tom is making a bet that the value of his residential property will increase over the year by more than the $6,321 it is costing him to hold the property. If it does, then he will post a profit in the form of positive equity growth. For Tom to achieve positive equity growth each year, he will need his residential property to increase in value each year by 1% ($6,321 / $631,000 = 1%).

In Australia, the residential property market has been growing in different suburbs at rates of five, ten or even 15% per year for the past decade, so investors in this asset class have experienced exceptional gains and would be pleased with their decision to leverage residential property as their engine of wealth. Tom is making the bet that his property will grow in value by more than 1% per year. This is justified given that residential property has increased by more than 3%p.a., even in poor years. A conservative 3% growth on his $600,000 property value equates to equity growth of $18,000 a year, leaving positive equity of almost $12,000. In a good year of 10% annual growth, the positive equity is almost $54,000.

Although residential property investment is a strong investment class, and one that has made many wealthy, it does have an eventual sting — market downturn. In the period 2003–2013, Australia experienced a Chinese-fuelled mining boom. One consequence was driving up house prices in Perth, the mining centre of Australia. Perth experienced annual house value increases exceeding 20%, and many investors jumped into that market. When iron ore prices plummeted in 2014, mining jobs were dumped, as were the houses. Perth experienced years of property value decline as a glut of properties was listed for sale.

If, for example, Tom purchased a residence in Perth prior to the decline, Tom's investment would record equity decline. These losses would be considered paper losses and would not be realised unless Tom sold the property for less than his $631,000 purchase price. What Tom would avoid is selling at a loss. Instead he, like most, would continue paying his mortgage because selling would only crystallise the loss and give him a debt against his name. For most, then, the chosen option is to wait until the residential property market rebounds.

The mathematics for investing in commercial property is quite different, yet quite simple. Investors who buy a shop do so for one reason — to provide a source of positively geared income. Investors will not be living in their shops; they are not purchasing them to be near their friends nor for the aesthetic beauty of the carpark out the front. Shops are purchased for the purpose of generating a positive cashflow and returning a profit to the investor.

Removing emotion from the purchase makes it a clear mathematical choice. I have come across several valuation methods for commercial property, however, by far the most common and well known valuation method is:

$$\text{Shop Value} = \frac{\text{Net Rent}}{\text{Rate of Return}}$$

Shop Value   Is the price paid or offered for the shop

Net Rent   Is the gross shop income less all the regular expenses such as council rates, water rates, repairs and maintenance, agents' fees and annual fire inspections

Rate of Return This is the rate the buyer wants to receive per year on the money as a decimal fraction. My target of a 7.5% rate of return is represented as 0.075.

I use a rate of return of 7.5% as a starting rate to determine the value of an investment property. Often called the capitalisation rate, 7.5% has, for many years, been used as an industry norm by real estate agents and investors to determine the value of a commercial property. Today the stock market and residential market are trading at record highs, which concerns investors and is directing investment money into the commercial property market. The effect of this increased demand has forced prices up. Therefore, retail shops are currently trading at capitalisation rates below 7.5%. While we accept the market is elevated at present, our valuation method will remain at a capitalisation rate of 7.5% to estimate a property's value. For me, this has been an unwritten industry norm since I started investing 20 years ago.

Today I can borrow money from the bank at around 4%. Hence the delta from our 7.5% capitalisation rate is 3.5%, being our income return or profit. More on this calculation later.

Let me demonstrate this again through another real-world example. Joanne runs a small café. Her landlord has listed the building in which she operates for sale. The landlord is asking $450,000. Using our valuation formula, we can determine if the landlord's asking price is close to our target rate of return.

Joanne's Café

Shop size   50m²

Lease Term   Five years with a five-year option. She is one year into that first five-year lease.

Gross Rent $40,000 per annum

Expenses $9,000 p.a. (incl. council rates, water, agents' fees, maintenance, fire inspections)

$$\textbf{Shop Value} = \frac{\text{Net Rent (\$40,000 - \$9,000) = \$31,000}}{\text{Rate of Return 0.075 (7.5\%)}} = \textbf{\$ 413,333}$$

The landlord's asking price of $450,000 is more than our valuation of the property. If we were to pay this asking price, the requested rate of return is:

$$\textbf{Return} = \frac{\text{Net Rent}}{\text{Value}} = \frac{\$31,000}{\$450,000} = \textbf{6.8\%}$$

If you were heading to an auction to buy the commercial premises where Joanne's Café operates, you would only want to bid up to $410,000 - $415,000. In doing so, however, you are not taking into account other factors or variables that may increase or decrease the shop's value. These are explained in later chapters.

If you did manage to secure the property for $413,000, then, according to our formula, you will have purchased the property at a capitalisation rate of 7.5%. The mathematics on this investment's income is not over at this point, however, because when considering your profit and cashflow your true capitalisation rate would not be 7.5%. You also need to allow for purchase costs. These can be significant, so they need to be factored in.

As a guide you should allow the following purchase costs for Joanne's Cafe:

Stamp Duty (this tax varies by State, but it averages around 3.6%) $ 15,000
Legal Fees (depends on property size and level of due diligence) $ 7,500
Total Purchase Cost   **$ 22,500**

I always like to add on these costs to understand the "true capitalisation rate" of the investment. Looking again at the rate of return for Joanne's Café, bought for $413,000:

Purchase Price $413,000
Purchase Costs $ 22,500
Total Purchase Price   **$435,000**

$$\text{Shop Value} = \frac{\text{Net Rent}}{\text{Rate of Return}}$$

OR

$$\text{Rate of Return} = \frac{\text{Net Rent}}{\text{Shop Value}}$$

In this case, the true capitalisation rate would be:

$$\text{Rate of Return} = \frac{\$31{,}000 \text{ Net Rent}}{\$435{,}000 \text{ Purchase Cost}} = 7.12\%$$

Therefore, by securing the café for $413,000, your true return would be 7.12%. In essence, the property will return you 7.12% on your borrowed money. This is akin to investing the $413,000 in the bank and receiving 7.12% interest.

Your goal is a positively geared source of income. To complete this purchase, you would attempt to secure the $435,000 funds as a loan from the bank. Of course, as with residential purchases, the bank will seek equity as security. The current interest rates are between 3.9–4.5%. Assume that you secure the loan at 4.3% for a property earning 7.12% return on that money. Your profit would be (7.12–4.3%) = 2.82% on the entire $435,000 purchase price. In essence, you are making a profit of ($435,000 x 0.0282), which is $12,267 per year.

For this example, I am assuming 100% of the purchase price is borrowed. If you contribute a deposit, you would increase this profit/income amount.

This café building is an asset that grows in capital value, and most markets would expect a 3–5% annual growth. Therefore, this shop returns an income of $12,267 each year, plus equity growth (3% on the $413,000 shop would equal $12,390). You can see why I get so excited each time I add a commercial property to my portfolio. They are solid and secure, add to my disposable income (it is indexed to grow), and provide a capital return should I ever sell. This is a true engine of wealth.

Competition to purchase is constant, and buyers will want to pay more, just as in the world of residential property.

Using Joanne's Café as an example, the following are key factors or variables that may drive the value of a shop up or down:

1) The café may be right on the beach with sensational views and a lot of people passing by. Highly visible and desirable locations mean buyers will accept a lower return, knowing that they can potentially push the rent up when the lease expires. Capitalisation rates may fall in these circumstances, dropping returns below 7%. My advice is to seek properties that are not in the CBD or on the beach if you want higher returns. Many years ago, early in my wealth-building process, interest rates were well over 10%. Given our cal-

culations above, you do not want to be aggressive or fall in love with a certain shop, resulting in a rate of return that is not sufficient to cover the interest payments to the bank. There will always be other properties.

2) The café may have a 10-year lease, offering buyers excellent security, or be part of a national chain, like The Coffee Club. This often drives the purchase price up and your rate of return down.

3) The café is on one of the city's busiest streets or opposite a train station where thousands of people walk by each day. Again, buyers will see value in the property's letting potential and overall security and will be prepared to pay more.

4) The café has a lease with an annual rent increase built in. Leases typically specify an annual rent increase between CPI (currently 2.1%) and 5%. The higher the annual increase, the more attractive the property.

5) The property is set on a large land-holding, and it may have greater re-development value.

Forces that drive shop values down:

1) The café is in a quiet country town with many other shops available for rent in the area.

2) The number of customers walking past each day is minimal, and the centre itself is not thriving.

3) The current tenant only has six months left on their lease and they may not stay on after the lease expires, creating a possible vacancy. Obviously, the success of a new tenant is never assured. I have benefitted when a tenant left, but a short lease going in should mean a reduction in your purchase price.

4) The shop is vacant, hence is not a "going concern". In Australia, a vacant possession is attractive for owner-occupiers looking to start a business, but not for investors as they must pay a 10% GST on the purchase price. You could build the 10% into your offer price, but for me this cost, plus the risk of having to locate an attractive tenant

in an unfamiliar location, means I recommend staying away from any shop that is vacant. Vacant shops account for roughly 20% of shops available for sale at any time.

We will cover more on specific property features in following chapters.

As demonstrated above, commercial properties are valued and purchased according to variations on a mathematical formula that is designed to provide the investor with a positively geared return. In the example above, we purchased the building housing Joanne's Café and, in doing so, created a positively geared income of $12,267 per annum. That is additional income with which you can choose to pay down your domicile home loan where you are unable to claim a tax deduction, or you can direct it to the café loan, and reduce your deductible loan level. Both will help increase the available equity base for your next property investment.

Borrow and Scale

Finally, the main reason I recommend retail property investing as the basis of your wealth-building engine and the key to your investment strategy is that it allows you, as an investor, to borrow and scale. Using our examples with Tom and Joanne, we can demonstrate the borrowing and scaling ability of residential versus commercial investments.

Earlier, we looked at Tom's purchase of a residential house and the negative-gearing aspects of that investment. Negative gearing is the catch cry of residential investors who will corner you at a party and discuss at length the benefits of investing in residential property. Most of them will consider themselves experienced in property investment and tell you just how much tax they are saving through a negatively-geared property. I consider that these party-goers are attracted to the short-term capital growth drug. My approach to building wealth involves a long-term (20+ years) investment strategy that manages risk to sustain you until you die, and then support your family thereafter.

To put residential investment simply, negative gearing means you are losing money to gain capital. Your investment property must have capital growth each year to offset that loss and provide a profit. The profit then appears in the form of increased equity, which is trapped in the value of the property. Meaning you must be able to sustain the negatively-geared loss from your income each year until you sell.

In Tom's residential investment example, he lost $6,321 per year on his $631,000 property. That doesn't seem a lot on one property, but a wealth engine needs multiple properties to sustain a family. It is the compounding effect of this loss when you acquire many properties that can bring the investor undone and prevent the continued growth of their portfolio.

Let's roll forward two or three years from Tom's first investment property. It would have increased in value, potentially providing him the ability to leverage that equity and buy a second investment property. Assuming Tom acquires a second residential investment property with similar characteristics to the first, it is logical that he would now be losing 2 × $6,321 per year, or $12,642 a year. Tom's bank may still be comfortable with his ability to service the two mortgages while carrying these losses and, if so, would approve his request to acquire a second investment property expanding his portfolio, given his day-to-day income is sufficient to sustain the annual losses.

Let's assume Tom waits another three years for his equity in both properties to grow. Once Tom's equity had built up enough, he is able to buy his third residential investment property. Again, if we assume this property has similar characteristics to the others, Tom would now be 3 × negatively geared or losing 3 × $6,321 = $18,963 each year.

The Australian Dream for our parents still remains "to own our domicile home"[3], yet only a small percentage, 8%, go on to buy a second residential property as an investment. Less than 2% of the Australian population buy a third residential investment and less than 1% own more than five residential properties. For those like Tom who do, banks become the debt police. Tom will need to justify that he can carry the negatively-geared losses resulting from multiple properties. By the time Tom accumulates five residential properties, he will be 5 × $6,321 = $ 31,605 negatively geared each year. If Tom is successful in servicing this debt and convincing the bank to continue to lend him more money, he may just be able to make it to six residential properties before the bank drops the hammer and refuses to lend him anymore. Unless you have inherited wealth or endless equity, job security is no longer a given and banks do not want to be exposed to an individual unable to service their negatively-geared losses.

Negatively-geared Residential Property Portfolios

Negatively-geared residential property investment was my experience before I learnt a better way to build wealth. I, like Tom, had collected five residential properties and was approximately 5 x 6,321 = $31,605 p.a. negatively geared. Over the 9–10 years I accumulated this asset portfolio, I also continued to climb the corporate ladder, achieving increases in salary. I thought the gearing was manageable. However, my bank did not! As I became

---

[3] A 2017 ABC study highlighted that the multiplier of the average salary to buy an average home has increased from 4 times in 1990 to 12 times in 2017, resulting in just 26% of millennials achieving home ownership. From Chau, David. 'Australian property "severely unaffordable", Sydney crowned "second least affordable market"' [online], ABC News, 23 January 2018.

more and more cashflow negative, the risk to the bank increased as my mortgage debt grew with each added property. In my case, at five properties, my mortgage was in the multi-millions and the bank considered me an unacceptable risk for several reasons.

The bank considered my position as too negatively-geared and, in their eyes, they were no longer prepared to allow me to draw up my loans to their maximum 80% LVR allowance to secure additional properties. While I had five tenants helping me with the mortgage repayments, I remember the bank manager asking me, "Phil, how will you pay the mortgage if all the tenants move out?" This seemed a strange question. I replied, "There is no chance all of my tenants would move out on the same day."

I remember his sobering reply, "None of your tenants have leases longer than six months. None of them have any significant security, and I can site countless examples of entire towns experiencing hardship when the mining company moved out, the auto company closed down, or the one major factory closed its operations."

He was right. I was totally reliant on my tenants paying their rent, and I was reliant on keeping my job to pay the $31,605 per year in negatively-geared expenses. Although I rationalised that my tenants were geographically and economically independent, and hence would not all leave together, the bank reminded me that even if half of them moved out, I would suffer financial stress and potentially be unable to meet my home mortgage repayments. Trying to convince a bank that their "risk calculator" on my lending was wrong, was akin to talking to a wall, so, my borrowing ability came to a dead stop.

With five residential properties and over $2 million of debt secured against these properties, the bank felt that their exposure

to me was significant. They declined any funding for future ac-
quisitions. My property portfolio was as big as it was going to get
because the bank had effectively put a lid on any future growth
plans. Don't get me wrong. I was proud that my equity each year
was growing faster than I could possibly save, and that I had
secured five residential houses that were working for me. I had
achieved a type of financial orbit where my equity was increasing
each year faster than I was spending.

However, the diagram on the following page illustrates the
"downward spiral" that occurs when accumulating negatively-geared properties. Although owning five properties is significant
for an individual, bank lending for residential property does not
provide the ability to scale and keep expanding your property
portfolio. At some point, you will reach the centre in which the
bank decides "no more".

COLLECTING NEGATIVELY GEARED PROPERTY

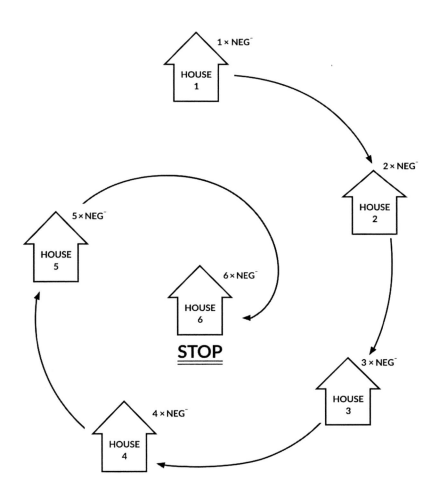

Most people in my place would have put the "cue in the rack", sat back, and watched the equity growth provide comfort for their future. My bank manager was right. My tenant's short-term leases and my reliance on my job meant that I was bearing the heavy burden of risk. I was losing sleep at night whenever the local or global economy took a downward turn.

Positively Geared Commercial Property Portfolios

Let us change gears and spiral out as we review a positively geared commercial property portfolio. As stated earlier, the price at which we aim to buy our investment shops is calculated as follows:

$$\text{Shop Value} = \frac{\text{Net Rent}}{\text{Rate of Return}}$$

Previously, we reviewed the purchase of the shop housing Joanne's Café, using the above formula. We generated a $12,267 annual positively geared profit on a $435,000 purchase price. Let's say that, after three years, you buy a second property as your equity has grown due to the capital growth of the building. Remember that the shop value, as defined by the above formula, is tied to the Net Rent, which has been increasing each year due to the inbuilt annual rent increases in the lease. Also, I would encourage you to combine the shop's positively geared profit with some of your personal savings, and pay down your loans further, increasing your available equity.

If you have debt on a property you live in, however, this is the loan you should pay down first for two reasons: a domicile property loan is not tax deductible and, secondly, the bank has an LVR of 80% on residential property, but only 65–70% on commercial property, so, paying down a residential loan increases your overall borrowing capacity.

After you purchase your second commercial property, assuming it has similar characteristics to the first, you will now be 2 × $12,267 positively geared = $24,534 per year. Just like the residential example above, over the next 2–3 years, you continue to benefit from those inbuilt annual rent increases, which now occur on both properties and, if you combine your positively geared cashflow of $24,534 with your personal savings, soon you will have built up the required equity to secure your third engine of wealth.

Once you secure the third shop in your portfolio, you will be generating 3 × $12,267 = $36,801 per year of positively geared income, and your equity will be growing at a faster rate. Remember, this positively geared income is treated the same as other income by the tax office, hence you will need to pay tax on it. However, due to depreciation benefits and other deductions from the shops, the tax burden is lower than payroll tax, leaving a significant sum for you to channel into further loan reductions. The fuel you now have available for your wealth engine is your equity, growing at a rate that enables you to secure your fourth property after just two years, instead of three.

If you continue this process and keep buying additional properties, in approximately five more years you will be looking at securing your sixth commercial property, generating more than 6 × $12,267 = $73,602 of positive cashflow per year!

For the purposes of this example, we have assumed each subsequent property had similar characteristics to the first, so, staying with that assumption, you would now have loans totalling $435,000 × 6 = $2,610,000. When I went to buy my sixth negatively geared residential property, the bank said that I was too negatively-geared and would be unable to pay the loans. At the time, I felt my wealth-building dreams had been hijacked by a banker!

When I had six shops with over $2.6 million in debt and an annual positive income of $73,600, secured by leases over 3–7 years, the conversations with my bank on acquiring the 7th, 8th and 9th properties were much nicer discussions, with the bank keen to continue lending me money.

Each shop held was positively geared at 7% or more, with the earlier shops returning 8–9%, given annual rental increases in the lease. In our previous example, you would have $73,000 per year additional income to add to your day job. The bank would place a big tick against your name from an income and cashflow perspective, and you would exceed their "income cover" measures used to determine your ability to repay the loan. You can see that a strategy to secure sufficient, ongoing income to enable you to retire and live off the proceeds can be achieved by having retail shops. That is a journey worth taking!

The bottom line is that your bank will see your portfolio and will be delighted by its strong cashflow positive position, and they will be impressed by the Weighted Average Lease Expiry (WALE), which we will cover in later chapters — this is a measure of the lease terms you have in place.

The following illustrates the "outward spiral" achieved by accumulating positively geared commercial property. There is no limit and, the more you have, the more they contribute equity for the next.

COLLECTING POSITIVELY GEARED PROPERTY

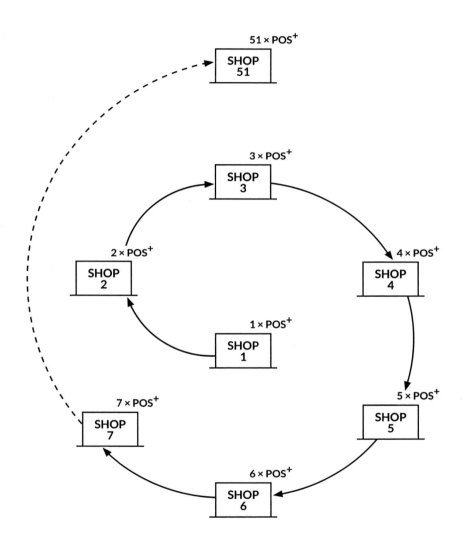

Before we start getting too excited about the thought of accumulating high-performance wealth engines, we need to understand some of the risks for commercial shops. One question I am regularly asked is:

"Can you afford the loans if one or all of the tenants move out?"

The answer here is no different from the answer in the world of residential property: No! However, there is a major difference between commercial and residential tenants. Residential tenants can be more transient and sign shorter, 6–12 month leases. When you are borrowing, banks will look at your ability to re-pay loans under circumstances of high vacancy, which is a higher risk with short, residential leases. Also, as most residential tenants do not own their own home, they tend to have less security to offer as a guarantee against future rent payments. If, for example, they lost their job residential tenants may default on rent.

Compare that to your position with commercial property investment. In this asset class, tenants tend to sign much longer three, five, ten or even 15-year leases. So, signing long leases offers banks the security of knowing that the location and site is secure for the next 5–10 years, and, if the commercial tenant leaves, they must continue paying rent until a new tenant is inserted. Furthermore, if a shop tenant defaults, they put at risk their guarantee, which is their place of residence. In many cases, retail tenants are entrepreneurial, and own their own home, providing you and the bank excellent security over future rental payments. Couple that security with the fact that commercial leases are longer in term and usually staggered over different expiry dates, and we have an asset class that offers the bank excellent security.

Another question I get on managing shops is:

"How do you maintain and support multiple properties that are geographically dispersed?"

For commercial property, maintenance costs are significantly lower than costs for residential property. As previously outlined, a shop typically has three solid brick walls, a concrete floor and a glass shop front, so there is not a whole lot that can go wrong that is your responsibility. Also, shop tenants want to provide their customers with a positive shopping experience, so the better operators go to great lengths to ensure that their shop fit-out is modern, clean, tidy and immaculately maintained to attract and please customers.

Commercial tenants largely manage maintenance and, when something needs repair or replacement, you can refer the tenant issue to the Body Corporate, if it is strata, or with the tenant's assistance engage a tradesperson to repair any fault. So, even if your properties are hundreds or thousands of kilometres apart, an annual inspection is all that is normally required.

As I indicated earlier, my partners and I own 51 positively geared commercial shops. These shops generate more than $700,000 per year of free cashflow after tax. I am securely leveraged, owing more than $14,000,000 to the bank on assets totalling $24,000,000. At present, I am waiting for our equity to grow before commencing negotiations with our bank to further expand our portfolio and purchase "one more shop". I find that there is always room for one more.

Commercial property investment can deliver the long-term wealth you seek. The following chapters will help you in your search to secure the best shop. There are many details to consider, from location, tenant selection, expense and contract management, lawyers, agents, and more.

One of my best friends has a catch cry, gleaned from a famous song, "Who let the dogs out!" by the Baha Men. For us, this represents the day when we will free ourselves from the shackles of labour and escape to the life we want to live, not one we have to live. The wealth engine powered by commercial property investment provides us a secure, indexed income that one day will enable the "dogs to get out", and us to tell our bosses, "I no longer need to work for you. I now work for myself."

Chapter 3

REDEFINING THE AUSTRALIAN DREAM

We have considered three available investment options for building real wealth: cash, shares, and property. I explained why I believe that cash and shares are not suitable to form the basis of a long-term, wealth-building engine because they do not allow you to leverage large borrowings and are not stable enough to protect you from market fluctuations. I then detailed why positively geared commercial properties contained the right investment characteristics to become your chosen vehicle for creating an engine of wealth — this is the asset class around which you can build a future.

Those within investment circles seldom debate residential property versus commercial property because most investors are not exposed to commercial shops as an asset class. The sheer scale of residential investors compared with commercial investors is a key factor in the possibility for profit in this asset class. Most investors understand residential property because most of us were raised in a house or unit, rented or owned, and we were witness to the safety, grounding, and security a home provided our family. Many of us were taught from a young age that you need to save to buy your own home, for it will provide safety and security throughout your life. The "Australian Dream" passed down from parents to children is of home ownership.

Unfortunately, the economy and house prices have meant that the millennial generation (20–35 year-olds today) are resigning themselves to the fact that home ownership is no longer obtainable. Remember, the foundation for our commercial property wealth engine is to buy and leverage your place of residence.

Let's examine the problem. When I was 22 years old, I bought my first property in South Sydney. It was a two-bedroom unit for which I paid $115,000. Straight out of university, I was employed by a global technology firm, and I earned $30,000 per year. The unit I purchased cost approximately four times my annual salary. Rolling forward 30 years, my son Jake, a plumber on a salary of $75,000 per year, would need $800,000 to buy the same unit. That equates to more than 10 times his annual salary!

The salary multiplier to buy your home has jumped from 4 times to 10 times in a generation, making home ownership a distant dream for our children. Even if one chooses to move to rural or regional Australia where property is less expensive, the respective house price to salary ratio is still over seven times. This means that our children are staring down the barrel of a life of debt if they want to own a home. They will need borrowings of more than 10 times their average annual salary to achieve the same Australian Dream that the Baby Boomers and Gen X instilled in them.

For Jake to finance a residential property, he knows that the bank will lend to an LVR of 80%. LVR means the Loan to Value Ratio, and is defined by the following formula:

$$\text{LVR} = \frac{\text{Loan}}{\text{Value}}$$

Jake's pursuit of the two-bedroom unit in South Sydney, valued at $800,000, would require him to save a deposit of at least 20% equity to achieve an 80% LVR. Let's re-write the formula to see just how much deposit Jake would need:

$$\text{Loan} = \text{LVR (80\%)} \times \text{Value} = 0.8 \times \$800,000 = \$640,000$$

This means the bank would lend Jake $640,000 against the $800,000 unit he is considering buying. Jake would need to inject $160,000 of personal savings ($800,000 - $640,000 = $160,000), plus the legal fees and stamp duty of around $40,000. Jake needs a deposit of at least $200,000 to buy this modest two-bedroom unit.

Like most 23-year-olds, Jake does not have $200,000 in savings. For such a saving and on his current income, around $75,000p.a., it would realistically take him 10 years to save that sort of deposit. By that time, the property value would have also increased, moving it further from his reach. Some banks will consider lending up to 90% of a property's value, however, they charge a once-off expense for mortgage insurance, and I do not recommend this route.

Just as our generation used residential units as a stepping stone to a residential house, we must consider introducing another stepping stone for millennials. The journey to home ownership for those looking to build a deposit may become:

Buy a small retail shop → Leverage the equity to buy a residential unit → Leverage the unit's equity to buy a house

This redefines the Australian Dream, based on the economic realities of today and into the future. Introducing commercial property as a stepping stone to the residential market may become more common, until residential property ownership becomes more affordable. Investing in commercial property is still affordable, and it places you "in the market", with your investment returning an income, and its capital value growing each year. Commercial property can be purchased on sound, positively geared mathematical principles, and offers investors the safety, security, and equity growth needed to build a residential deposit.

The other options for securing a deposit for Gen X and millennials are:

1. Wait until the market returns to greater affordability
2. Wait for a residential property market crash, providing an opportunity to enter
3. The death of a wealthy relative, or
4. Win the lottery

Although we may experience a softening in property sales and a stagnant market for many years, a real change in affordability is not anticipated, leaving options three and four as the best hope. And, as my mentor tells me, "Hope is not a strategy!"

Unfortunately, for those market entrants awaiting a plummet in residential prices, I think you will be waiting a while. As 70% of residences are owner-occupied, this provides a natural barrier to a significant reduction in housing affordability, with the market more likely to sit flat for years to come.

In redefining the Australian Dream then, the first step in investing in commercial property is understanding what the banks want. The 1% of people who receive an inheritance or win the lottery can skip this section, the other 99% who need to borrow to procure their first investment shop should read on.

The demographics of a first buyer are not solely those aged in their 20–30s at the start of their wealth journey. Some 40–50 year olds who have built significant equity in their residences can leverage this to accelerate their wealth-building strategy. It is not uncommon in Australia that, after 20 years of work, with a laser focus on building equity in their own home, the Gen X's are blind to the potential of dormant equity. This was the experience of my co-author, Stephen. He only began investing in commercial property when he was 51, having built $1 million of idle equity within his domicile residence.

For Gen X's, like Stephen, who have managed to build equity in their residential home, this idle equity will help accelerate your first shop purchase. Let's say you bought a $650,000 home in an outer suburb of Sydney 10 years ago. Over the next decade, you have paid down the $520,000 bank loan by $220,000. In the meantime, the property value has increased to $1 million. That means you have $700,000 of equity available to leverage in purchasing a commercial property. We know from the previous example that banks will loan up to 80% of the value of a property (LVR = 80%). Therefore, in this case, $560,000 of equity can be used to procure a positively geared retail investment. I have often commented to friends about this "idle equity" sitting in their houses, letting them know it is akin to having a beautiful red Ferrari sitting in your garage and never bothering to drive it or even sit in it and rev it.

When it comes to securing commercial debt, the options are banks or mortgage brokers. Banks are the largest lenders, but are conservative with their lending principles, requiring you to jump over three hurdles to secure borrowing:

1) Loan to Value Ratio

Banks and brokers only lend to an LVR of 65–70% on commercial property. The LVR (or Loan to Value Ratio) means the amount of money you want the bank to lend you, divided by the valuation the bank's valuer places on the target property:

$$LVR = \frac{Bank\ Loan}{Property\ Value}$$

A common misconception is that the value of a commercial shop is the price the market is willing to pay, especially if sold at auction. That is not the case. If you think a shop is worth $500,000, the bank's valuer will more than likely think it is worth $450–470,000 because they will apply a vacancy factor, lowering the net rent. Other value-reducing factors I have experienced from bank valuers include:

- They don't like the area or the local demographics,
- They don't like the tenant mix, or
- They don't like the quality of the building's construction.

By reducing the valuation, the bank requires more equity from you to secure the loan. In short, the bank is ensuring you have more "skin in the game", hence less risk for them. In the Gen X example above, the $560,000 in available equity can be used in this LVR equation, hence accelerating your ability to reach the bank's LVR level of 65–70%.

The bank's aim is simple: to protect their money and remove risk from the transaction. So, keep a smile on your face when dealing with your bank regarding their valuation opinions and remember, one day many years from now, you will sell it and tell them exactly what the property is worth.

Once a valuation is received, the LVR offered by the bank becomes important. In residential property investments, the accepted LVR by banks is higher, typically 80%. This means that, if a property is valued at $500,000, the bank will lend you 80% of its value (being $400,000) and you need to contribute $100,000 to purchase it. In these times of low interest rates, banks will encourage buyers by lending 90% of the property value, but beware of LVRs of 90% or above.

LVRs above 80% mean the bank will require borrowers to take out mortgage insurance at a significant cost to the borrower, around $20,000–25,000, depending on the loan amount. This is designed to protect the bank's interests if you lose your job, go broke, or stop paying the mortgage. This insurance is expensive and provides you no security at all. It is paid by you and is only there to protect the bank. The bottom line is that you need to achieve the bank's LVR limit and avoid mortgage insurance.

The LVR position on commercial property is 70%, however, some banks are starting to ask for additional safety, and are pushing borrowers to 65%, meaning the other 35% of equity comes from the buyer. For our calculations, moving forward we will work on an LVR position of 70% as there are still banks offering this, and I suggest you keep asking until you find an institution offering 70%.

2) Interest Cover

The second hurdle banks put in your way is interest cover. Interest cover is a measure the banks use to ensure you have the financial capacity to pay the mortgage each month. The bank will take into account the income generated from rent you collect from tenants, and your salary. The total of that income must exceed the bank's target, typically 1.5 times the interest you will incur on borrowings.

If you work full-time, this measure is easily achieved with a positively geared shop. However, if you are retired, it can become problematic to expand your portfolio of positively geared investments.

3) Weighted Average Lease Expiry

The third hurdle the banks inflict is the WALE of your investment. The WALE is the Weighted Average Lease Expiry — it gives the bank an indication of how many years your rent is secured for. When buying an individual tenanted building, this calculation is relatively easy. For example, if you are buying a single shop with a hairdresser as a tenant who has a five-year lease and the hairdresser is 12 months into that lease, then the WALE is 4 years; that is the remaining term of the lease. When we are looking to buy a building with multiple tenancies, however, the bank will work out the total number of years left to run proportional to the total rent to determine their WALE figure. The longer the WALE, the happier your bank manager will be. Equally though, the shorter the WALE, the more perceived risk the bank will place on the loan. When banks sense higher risk, they may demand a lower LVR or, worse, inflict a higher interest rate on you, compensating them for the increased risk.

Like most conversations with a banker, there is little room for negotiation. My advice is that if the bank is introducing charges or hurdles that you consider transfer too much risk onto you, look for financing alternatives. Seeking advice from a mortgage broker is a good option as they do not typically represent any single financial institution.

In summary, my advice when dealing with banks or brokers is:

- Always be prepared to take your business across the road to another bank offering a better deal
- Banks are not your friends and will rarely offer a discount for having all your business with them
- When applying for a loan, always have another bank shadowing your application, so you can switch if needed
- Always ask them to improve their interest rate

As an example, when my co-author, Stephen, selected his first target shop and approached his existing bank, he also approached two others. Although that required completing three sets of loan paperwork, which was tedious, the benefit was worth the effort. For the same property, the three banks offered very different borrowing interest rates. The responses were 5.99%, 4.76%, and 4.2%, highlighting how banks use the different WALE and risk multipliers to determine their rates. The bank with the highest rate was sent packing. The next step was to indicate to the middle bank (Stephen's existing bank) that their competition was at 4.2% and, if they wanted to retain his business, they had to improve. The lowest rate was with a bank that had loan conditions that were not advantageous, hence Stephen's preference to get the middle bank to meet the market and lower their rate. In Stephen's case, he was able to secure a matching 4.2% rate from his preferred bank and create a borrowing foundation with the bank manager, which he is now leveraging for his second and third properties.

A Case Study

Understanding how to optimise the conversation with a bank provides critical input to securing your property. Let's use an example to demonstrate the LVR and WALE hurdles. I propose you buy a well-placed building, housing a small hairdressing salon. I personally love buying hair dressing salons, as people will always need a haircut and tenants want to stay in the area for a long time and therefore sign long leases. I will expand on what are the most attractive business types in later chapters.

If you are wondering where to look to find commercial properties for sale, they are in the real estate section of the weekly newspaper or, my preference, on the internet. The website *www. realcommercial.com.au* lists all available properties for sale or lease. You can refine your search to select retail shops in a certain area and price range. You can even specify shops with hairdresser tenants.

For a small 40m² hairdressing salon, the shop may be a strata title, meaning it is one shop in a larger building of many shops. In this case, there are 10 shops in the building, and the hairdresser represents only 8% of the strata floor space. The building is managed by a Body Corporate, which in essence is a representative group of owners appointed to manage the building. A Body Corporate can also be an external company appointed by the owners. As your shop is 8% of the total building by floor space, you would be liable for 8% of the building's maintenance and repair costs. These are called outgoings.

The financials for this shop are:

EXPENSES

Council Rates	$ 950	
Water Rates	$ 850	
Fire Inspection	$ 500	
Body Corporate fee's	$2,100	(This includes insurance, repairs and maintenance)
Total expenses	$4,400	

INCOME

Gross Rent	$31,220	per annum plus GST

You are therefore looking at a net rent position of $31,220 - $4,400 = $26,820 per annum.

Using our valuation formula described in Chapter 2:

$$\text{Value} = \frac{\text{Net Rent}}{0.075\ (7.5\%\ \text{return})} = \frac{\$26,820}{0.075} = \$357,600$$

You submit an offer to the owner at $340,000 and, after a few weeks of negotiation, an offer of $350,000 is accepted. Given this is a commercial property, your chosen bank will lend on a Loan to Value Ratio (LVR) of 70% or $245,000. Therefore, you will need a deposit of 30% of the total funds required to purchase the shop. Plus, you must include the purchase costs: State government stamp duty and legal expenses.

Stamp duty is a charge applied by State governments in Australia in relation to the transfer of land or property. The charge varies by State and can be easily calculated, using one of the many online stamp duty calculators. For your property, the stamp duty calculation is $11,586. Legal fees include conveyancing, title searches, and loan application fees, and vary depending on the complexity of the property being purchased and the level of due diligence required. For your single hairdresser shop, there is only one lease to review, so this is relatively straightforward. You should expect fees of around $7,500.

Your total purchase costs look like this:

Shop Purchase Price	$350,000
Stamp Duty	$ 11,586
Legal Fees	$ 7,500
Total Purchase Price	$369,086

Thus, the balance you need for your purchase is $369,086 – $245,000 = $124,086.

This case study suggests that you need to secure almost $125,000 to purchase an entry level retail shop. This is lower than the $200,000 for a residential unit in South Sydney, but still well beyond many individual's ability to save. So, back to the revised Australian Dream. How can a 20-something with no equity, or a 40-something with some equity in their home, start building their retail property investment wealth engine?

The answer is, find a friend. It is rare to partner with another for a share in a negatively-geared residential property, however, it is relatively easy to partner with others and share in positively geared commercial shop returns. This is what I did to get started. I partnered with two, like-minded friend investors, and we each chipped in equity. If we had started with this hairdressing shop, we would only need to secure $41,500 each to pursue this investment.

You may be asking, "How do I find a partner willing to invest $62,000 or two partners with $41,500 each?" Start with people you know, and work down the list. Ask your mother and father. If they have equity in their home, all you need is a little unused equity diverted towards this shop purchase. Some banks discourage adult children from leveraging their parents' house as equity on investments, citing the parent's age or stage in retirement as a mitigating risk.

Next, you could ask your siblings and friends. Although the barrier to entry has been reduced with the ability to readily split the shop returns, you still need like-minded investors willing to go on this wealth journey with you.

If you can't leverage a suitable partner or guarantor, then you are left with the starting hurdle of saving your entry deposit. In this situation, I recommend the stock market as a vehicle to grow your savings and deposit. If you only have $20,000, $30,000 or $40,000 saved, then shares often provide better returns than money in the bank earning 2% interest. The objective is to diligently invest your deposit in growth assets while continuing to contribute to additional savings.

Remember, the stock market is simply a tool to help grow your deposit faster; it is not your investment vehicle of choice, merely a stepping stone while building a deposit. Going in, you must recognise that the challenge of securing $125,000 from shares and savings will take a number of years. The strategy to build a long-term wealth engine will take 10–20 years more. The comfort you can take is that, after the first few years needed to secure the initial deposit, the second property will be easier and quicker. Not unlike your parents a generation ago as they chased the Australian Dream of home ownership, making sacrifices on holiday destinations and cutting back on entertainment is necessary to achieve your wealth ambitions.

A few months ago, I read the book *The Barefoot Investor* by Scott Pape. Pape covered the topic of securing a deposit. He stated that "many of us buy things we never really needed, never really desired, they were just spur of the moment impulsive purchases that a few months later are discarded because we never really needed them in the first place." Pape reflects that often we don't look back and judge ourselves on why we bought those items, and if we do they are justified to cheer us up or as "retail therapy". Pape indicates that a savings discipline is crucial to beginning an investment strategy and securing that first deposit. Because he knows, as do I, that once the snowball begins to roll down the hill, it will pick up speed, and wealth will accumulate with it.

Either through your savings or collecting one or two investment partners, once the deposit is accrued and the hairdressing salon is purchased, it will immediately produce positively geared returns, plus capital equity growth. Creating this partnership, allows you to begin the journey and start growing your investment, well ahead of waiting until you individually save the deposit. As I said, I took this approach with my first retail investment and today our partnership remains as strong as ever. Our investment group has survived 15 years and over 51 shops.

Now that you have secured the $124,086 in funds for the balance of the hairdressing shop investment, you must secure a bank or mortgage broker. As mentioned in Stephen's example, interest rates vary considerably across the major banks and credit unions. On smaller investment loans, credit unions and member institutions may provide more competitive interest rates, but you must also factor in account-keeping fees and other charges. Luckily for us, the federal government mandates that banks advertise their "true comparison rate", which is the rate with all their account-keeping fees and charges factored in, so don't be drawn into the headline rate — make sure you look at the comparison rate.

I use Bankwest and have found them consistently cheaper than the market over the past five years. I receive no commission or gratuity from Bankwest as a result of this recommendation. I would look at ING Direct also. In his book, Scott Pape recommends ING as they have competitive rates. The key here is to identify and work with your preferred lender, keeping them informed of the property you are trying to buy. Share the property sales material (usually an Information Memorandum) with details on lease terms, expiry dates, expenses, and so on.

Your bank manager will review the purchase, including key aspects of the investment, such as the quality of the tenant's business, how long they have been trading, the length of the lease, the amount of rent, your employment, number of years employed, and amount of income you earn. The bank will have their opinion of the area's demographics, population, and expected growth rates and vacancy rates. In most cases, banks require a formal valuation of the shop by one of their valuers. The good news in all this is that, when the bank comes back to you 1–2 weeks later and approves your loan, you can be assured they feel the investment is sound. This will re-enforce your own decision to buy the property in the first place.

So, we know your hairdresser shop costs just under $370,000. You secured or saved the $125,000 deposit and went to the bank asking them to lend you the 70% LVR or $245,000 against the shop. You know you qualify on the bank's 70/30 LVR measure, but do you qualify on their interest cover measure? The interest on a $245,000 loan at an interest rate of 5% would be (245,000 x 0.05) = $12,250. The bank requires you (and your partners) to have 1.5 times interest cover, so that would be (1.5 x $12,250) = $18,375. Given that the property will generate $26,820 per annum in net rent, you should be well covered on this measure, even before the bank factors in your personal income.

After reviewing your application, the bank approves your loan and confirms the interest rate. You should then call your solicitor, instructing them to proceed with purchase and settlement of the shop. I will expand on all of the property purchasing steps in later chapters.

Various commercial loan types are available to buyers. I will expand on these in later chapters, but for now let us assume that an "interest only" loan is requested and approved. Cashflow for the hairdressing salon involves rent of $31,220 per year. After paying expenses of $4,400 per year, you are left with a net rental income of $26,820p.a. You must also pay the bank their interest which, at 5% on $245,000, is $12,250 per year. You are left with $26,820 – $12,250 = $14,570 per year profit. Not bad! If you took on a partner, this profit would be split between you.

Before we start celebrating, we need to consider the tax man. Unfortunately, our $14,570 profit is considered income, so normal income tax rates apply. Assuming that you and your partners are on the 30-cents-in-the-dollar tax rate[4], your tax bill would be ($14,570 x 0.3) = $4,371, leaving you (and your partners) with a collective after-tax profit of $10,199 per annum. You are earning $196 per week while you sleep! It gets better. That income stream is indexed to inflation, as you will typically have CPI or 3% annual rent increases built into the lease when you purchase the shop.

You have now established your first engine of wealth, with your shop earning you $196 per week. This is akin to having a friend helping you get ahead in life as you work toward the Australian Dream of owning your own home. In the meantime, you are building a wealth engine with commercial property.

---

[4] Which is the Australian tax rate applicable for earnings up to $180,000 per annum

Over the next two to three years, your equity in the hairdressing shop will increase. During this time, your personal savings should be added to the shop's income and poured back into the loan, reducing your debt and increasing your equity. The forces of time are also working on the capital growth of the building — the shop value increases each year as you apply the rental increases built into the lease. Building equity now won't feel as difficult a task as it did while saving your deposit. You now have a tenant helping and a property in the market, which is increasing in value and producing a stream of positive cashflow.

Below is an image of what you have created, your first Engine of Wealth.

YEAR 1 START UP

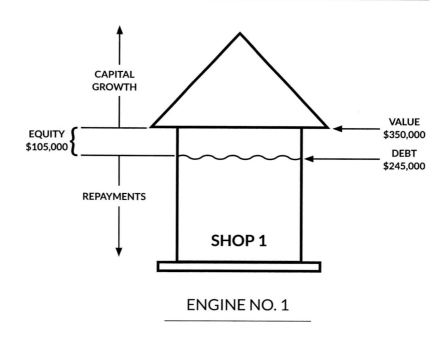

Upon settlement of your first shop, you should take a moment to be proud of what you have achieved. After the hard work and saving for that first deposit, it is now working for you, and, more importantly than that, the borrowed money is also working for you. However, building a long-term wealth engine means you must stay the course and adhere to the same savings culture you did while saving your deposit, this will ensure you accelerate your equity growth. A major lever to growing your equity involves allocating your savings along with the shop's $196 per week of positively geared income to paying down the loan. It's the combined strength of positive income, personal savings and capital growth that will quicken your equity growth, helping you reach the next goal — securing your second retail property!

Chapter 4

RIDE THE OUTWARD
SPIRAL TO WEALTH

Securing your first commercial property means you have done the hard work and your wealth-building strategy is underway as your first engine of wealth works for you. You saved for the deposit, and perhaps teamed up with a friend or two to secure a positively geared property, which is now adding to your income and accelerating you to the second investment property or your residence. Although it has been 15 years since I bought my first retail shop, I vividly recall watching the income flow in each month, and thinking, Wow! This is great! I can't wait to start looking for the next one.

The next question to ask is, "How much equity do I need to save before I can purchase another?" If you recall, in Chapter 2, I shared a graphic depicting the benefit of the ever-lasting outward spiral from buying commercial property. We reflected that if you remain disciplined with saving, together with the shop's rent growing each year, the equity builds. The more properties you purchase, the more powerful the wealth engine becomes and the quicker you move on to the next property.

When we redefined the Australian Dream, we detailed the benefit of purchasing a retail shop to leverage the positively geared income in order to buy a residential unit or house to live in. After 1–2 years of retail shop-driven equity growth, you need to decide whether the next property transaction is a unit to live in, or whether you should keep renting and buy another shop. I can't help with home ownership timing, but I can help with the economic value of pursuing a second retail shop.

There are four sources of equity growth after you secure your first shop. The first is your monthly savings, set aside from your living expenses. Second comes the positively geared income available after paying the loan interest and expenses (in the hairdresser's case, $196 per week). Third comes the annual rent increases built into the lease. The fourth and final source of equity growth is the capital growth in the asset, driven by rent increases. All of these are now being leveraged to build equity, assisting you to secure your next shop.

To understand how equity can be accrued to buy a second shop, I will use another example. The average Australian working couple has a combined annual income of $100,000 per year. After paying living expenses, tax, rent, food, car and other outgoings, you may be able to save $12–15,000 per year. Saving $1,000 per month is a good target to reduce the mortgage on your first shop.

I will continue, assuming that you and your investment partner from the hairdresser are keen to invest together again, thereby each saving $12,000 per year. If you are investing by yourself, the strategy remains the same — it will just take a little longer to save enough equity for the next purchase. By adding your savings to the positively geared income from Shop #1, that is $196 x 52 = $10,192 per year, you will reduce your annual mortgage by $24,000 + $10,192 = $34,192. This provides $34,192 of equity in the property from your tenant's year 1 rent and your personal savings.

Every year the rent increases, in accordance with the lease terms. Increases vary between leases from CPI (Consumer Price Index) to 5%. My starting position for annual increases is 3%p.a., that figure is my bottom line with tenants. Of course, during lease renewal negotiations or tenant changeover, you can raise it to 4 or even 5%, and this is not uncommon. For the purpose of our hairdresser example, we will maintain a 3% annual rent increase.

Using CPI is my least favourite index for rental increases as several published versions of CPI exist, leading to confusion as to whether a monthly, quarterly or annual figure should be used. To avoid confusion and to protect against a situation where CPI tracks below market rents, start with a 3%p.a. rental increase. If you can get your tenants to accept 4–5%, then do so. Remember, it is a negotiation — the tenant does not have to renew their lease with you.

Factoring in the third source of equity growth (from a 3% annual rent increment), means that, at the end of year 1, the rent increases from $26,820 (x 1.03) to $27,624. Remember, this increase is cumulative over the years, while mortgage repayments should remain static at $12,250 per year. In later chapters, we will discuss the types of bank loans and interest options to pursue.

The table below indicates how much additional income is contributed to available equity through annual rent increments. After four years, the additional rent flowing into your savings totals $2,486:

Year 1 Rent	$26,820	Net Additional Rent
Year 2 Rent	$27,624	$804
Year 3 Rent	$28,452	$828
Year 4 Rent	$29,306	$854

The fourth source of equity unleashes the power of capital growth. Calculating this, involves revisiting our valuation formula to determine the new property value with the added equity from rent increments:

$$\text{Property Value} = \frac{\text{Net Rent}}{\text{Rate of Return}}$$

or

$$\text{Rate of Return} = \frac{\text{Net Rent}}{\text{Property Value}}$$

Our hairdresser was purchased for $350,000 with an annual Net Rent of $26,820. This means our hairdresser secured a Rate of Return of 7.66%. Roll forward a year to the next lease anniversary. Apply the rent increase of 3%, i.e. $26,820 × 1.03 = $27,624 in Year 2. As shown below, the overall value of the property and hence the equity you can leverage for your next purchase has increased from $350,000 (Year 1) to $360,861 in just 12 months:

$$\text{Property Value} = \frac{\text{Net Rent}}{0.0766} = \frac{\$27,624}{0.0766} = \$360,861$$

Increasing our rent by 3% per year results in an additional $804 in rent in Year 2. In the eyes of other investors and your banker, this has added ($360,861 - $350,000) = $10,861 to the value of your building in that year.

Looking at the total equity you are building each year from your savings, positively geared income, and capital growth you have:

Savings (2 partners)	$24,000
Positive Shop Income	$10,192
Future Rental Increment	$ 800
Capital Appreciation	$10,861
Equity Growth per annum	$45,853

Without a retail property investment, your individual savings would be $12,000. Imagine saving $45,000 per year. This is how easy it is to quickly expand your wealth engine and equity base. Using our earlier calculations, after four years of saving and equity growth, you have over $180,000 of available equity. You can now understand my passion for the power of positively geared commercial property as the engine for equity growth and wealth.

The objective to secure your second investment property is now not as daunting. In fact, after just four years, you will have enough equity to approach the bank and ask for a second investment loan to secure Shop #2. Let's revisit our example of the $350,000 hairdressing salon. The salon has been appreciating at 3% per annum for 4 years. Its value over that period looks like this:

Year	Value	Net Rent (3% annual increases)
1	$350,000	$26,820
2	$360,861	$27,624
3	$371,445	$28,453
4	$382,592	$29,306

After four years, we can assume that the value in the market of the second shop we are considering to purchase would have also increased. Let's assume that target Shop #2 is valued at $400,000 and that the net rent is $30,000, equating to a 7.5% return. Remember, this return is without the sales costs, like stamp duty, legal fees, and bank application fees. I will expand on several negotiation techniques to help improve your rate of return in later chapters, but, for now, we will stick with explaining our wealth-building strategy.

The purchase cost for Shop #2 would be as follows:

Shop Purchase Price	$ 400,000
Stamp Duty	$ 13,768
Legal Fees	$ 8,500
Total Purchase Price	**$422,268**

After four years of equity growth, it is time to revisit the bank to seek their approval on a new loan. This time, however, you will seek a loan for the entire amount, using your first investment property as equity to support this loan. In other words, the equity and savings applied to paying down Shop #1's mortgage is now the deposit for Shop #2.

The bank is holding the title for Shop #1. You need the property valuation to reflect the equity captured over 4 years of saving. Our calculation suggests that you have built equity of $45,000 × 4 years = $180,000 and that Shop #1 should be valued by the bank and investors at $382,500. Next, we must calculate if the $180,000 in saved equity is sufficient for the $422,268 needed to buy Shop #2.

Using the same Loan to Value Ratio (LVR), 70/30, the bank should loan you $400,000 x 0.7% = $280,000. This means you need equity of $422,268 – $280,000 = $142,268 to secure your second property. With your investment partner and four years of saving, you can add Shop #2 to your portfolio, and have roughly $37,000 of excess equity. Well done! This excess is a great starting point for your third investment property.

Four years is a long wait, and property investing can be boring at times while we wait for equity to build, but, like the tortoise and the hare, patience pays off. Time is key to creating real, long-lasting wealth. Sure, you could grow wealth quicker on the share market, but, like the hare, at some point the market will tire and your asset base will be at risk. The good news is that things do speed up as you begin to collect more properties and harness the collective power of their combined capital growth and positive cashflow. I like to think of this as moving through the gears of your wealth engine.

We know that Shop #2 is possible. I want to expand on the conversation with the bank manager for the property. You and your investment partner will present your plans for a $422,268 investment loan. The principles have not changed. Banks will consider how you stack up against their 70/30 LVR lending position — except that this time it won't just be on one property — you will be measured against two properties. We know that the original loan for Shop #1 was $245,000 and that, over four years, the mortgage has reduced by $35,000 x 4 = $140,000. Note that the $10,861 in annual capital appreciation is not applied to your mortgage — only equity that you can draw upon with Shop #2. Therefore, your mortgage position with the bank on Shop #1 after four years has reduced to $105,000.

There are a few variables I have not included, which may make your asset position even stronger after four years. Firstly, your monthly interest payment on Shop #1 would have reduced as you paid down your mortgage. Secondly, it is highly likely that you and your investment partner's income has increased over the years, allowing for increased savings. Factoring in these saving advantages, the $105,000 could be as low as $70,000–80,000. For simplicity, I have not included these opportunities for further saving, so we remain conservative on your asset and equity position.

The bank's LVR calculation for both shops would look like this:

$$LVR = \frac{\text{Total Bank Loans}}{\text{Total Property Value}}$$

$$= \frac{\$105,000}{\underset{\$382,592}{\text{Shop \#1}}} + \frac{\$422,268}{\underset{\$400,000}{\text{Shop \#2}}} = \frac{\$527,268}{\$782,592} = \mathbf{67\%}$$

This is an excellent outcome from four years of saving. Banks will consider this an attractive proposition, as the combined LVR is less than 70%. Therefore, apart from the usual comments from the bank around "lower property valuations and the security of your base salary", there should be no trouble in finalising the loan and securing Shop #2.

Well done!

Let's consider a hypothetical. What if the LVR was 71%? This would occur if you and your partner had not saved quite as much each year, or you started looking for the second shop after 3.5 years instead of four. Your bank manager won't be overly impressed with a 71% LVR to purchase the second investment shop because this is above their lending criteria. You may receive an immediate "No". If so, you may need more time for Shop #1 and your savings to grow because, in six months, you will have paid off another $12,000 of your loan.

Not all banks will put the brakes on at 71%. They may want to include some risk conditions, given your existing loan business with them. I have had conversations for shop purchases with an LVR around 73%. My bank was willing to take on a higher LVR at the start of the loan on the condition that the positively geared income from the shops would be ploughed back into the loan, quickly driving the LVR below their target 70/30 position within one or two years.

Recapping the hurdles to bank approval: at 67%, the LVR hurdle is cleared. The next hurdle is the interest cover measure. The loans for our two sample properties now total $527,268. At 5% interest, you would pay $26,363 per year. The bank requires a 1.5 times interest cover, which equates to $39,545 per year. Your net rents are $29,306 for Shop #1 and $30,000 for Shop #2, totalling $59,306 per year. Net rents from the two shops adequately cover this interest measure — even without adding your combined income and savings.

After waiting 2–3 weeks for bank approvals, you get a call back from your bank manager approving your loan. You are now free to purchase your second investment property. Like before, you call your solicitor and arrange for settlement to commence. Soon, you are the proud owner of two retail shops, joining a small segment of the population who own more than one investment property.

You are now in command of over $527,000 of the bank's money, and control properties worth $782,000. The following is a diagram of your investment portfolio after four years:

4 YEARS IN

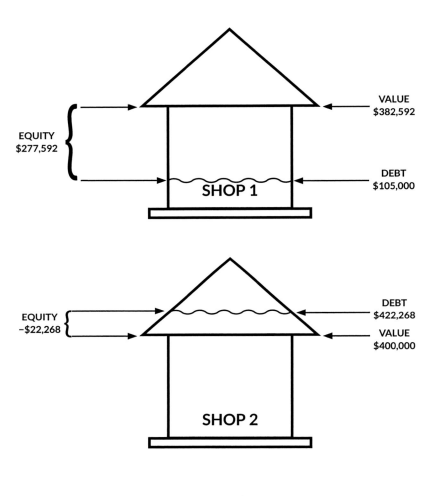

$$\text{LVR} = \frac{\text{TOTAL DEBT} \quad \$527,268}{\text{TOTAL VALUE} \quad \$782,592} = 67\%$$

TWO ENGINES ONLINE

With your second shop or engine of wealth online, we should re-examine what's happening with your cashflow and hence your ability to build equity. The shops rent for $59,306. Interest on your debt totals $26,363 annually. Therefore, your taxable profit totals ($59,306 - $26,363) = $32,943. As we know from Shop #1, you must pay income tax. Assuming that you are still in the 30% tax bracket, you will pay $9,883 in tax, leaving you (and your investment partner) a $23,060 after-tax profit to channel into loan reductions.

Given I like to stop and smell the roses after each purchase, celebrate that you now have two investment retail shops working for you, generating over $23,000 a year in after-tax profit — that is $443 a week in your pocket. Bear in mind that your equity growth is not only these positively geared profits; you also have two shops and their rents, appreciating in value. With properties worth $782,592 and an assumed (conservative) market appreciation of 3% per year, you will also enjoy capital growth of $782,592 x 3% = $23,477 a year!

Before we load up and prepare for the third property, there is one further upside that we have not covered. When a lease expires, you, the landlord, are entitled to apply a "market adjustment" to the rent. In short, this brings the hairdresser's rent into line with other shops in the area. You purchased your hairdresser one year into a five-year lease. Hence, in Year 4, they are due for a lease extension and a market adjustment of their rent.

This solid 3% return is far lower than the exaggerated 15–20% annual increase that residential properties experienced in Sydney, Melbourne, and Perth from 2010–2015. As mentioned earlier, as a safe tortoise, I prefer retail properties, as opposed to the handcuffed hares who invest in only a handful of residential homes.

Market adjustments move rents in the landlord's favour — only once in 15 years have I experienced a downward adjustment. However, to remain as conservative as possible, I have not included any step change in assumed rents due to "market adjustments". This means that the LVRs and valuations for the shops would be higher in the real world.

As we start Year 5, if you maintain your savings plan, individually or with your investment partner, you have the following equity growth:

Combined Savings	$24,000	
Positive Shop Income	$23,060	
Future Rental Increment	$ 1,800	($900 is the average rent increment per year per shop)
Capital Appreciation	$23,477	
Equity Growth per annum	**$72,337**	

Wow! This is independent too of annual rent increments. You can see the power of selecting an investment strategy founded on retail property. It is very difficult to save $72,000 in a year, or even $36,000 for each investment partner, yet you will have achieved this annual equity growth in under five years.

Perhaps you can understand why one of my favourite sayings is a quote from Oliver Twist, "Please, can I have some more?" As before, a third property requires the power of time. By now, however, your equity is building at twice the rate it did in the first four years, so you will build the equity required to secure your third investment at a much faster rate.

To demonstrate this, let's extend your example portfolio and see what happens after waiting three more years. A long time you say, however, while you are waiting, you keenly watch the market and learn more about property and tenant management through hands-on experience while maintaining your disciplined savings culture.

The table below shows the property value of your initial $350,000 hairdressing salon, growing at 3%p.a. Through rental increases built into your lease. The table below illustrates the Year 5 rent and valuation, if we apply the market adjustment mentioned above.

Year	Net Rent @ 3%	Property Value (@7.66% RoR)	Possible Net Rent with 5% Year 5 Adjustment	Property Value post Market Adjustment
1	$26,820	$350,000		
2	$27,624	$360,861		
3	$28,453	$371,445		
4	$29,306	$382,592		
5	$30,185	$394,060	$32,705	$426,965
6	$31,091	$405,882	$33,686	$439,767
7	$32,023	$418,055	$34,697	$452,958

After seven years, Shop #1's valuation is over $34,000 higher, if we apply the market adjustment in Year 5. The table below details the same calculations, but for Shop #2, purchased in Year 4. Note that Shop #2 was purchased with a Rate of Return of 7.5%.

Year	Net Rent @ 3%	Property Value (@ 7.5% RoR)
5	$30,000	$400,000
6	$30,900	$412,000
7	$31,827	$424,360

At the end of Year 7, let's assume your target Shop #3 is another similar retail shop although slightly dearer than the others, costing $490,000. The net rent for Shop #3, at a 7.5% Rate of Return, is $36,750.

Purchase costs on your third commercial property would be:

Shop #3 Purchase Price	$ 490,000
Stamp Duty	$ 17,813
Legal Fees	$ 9,000
Total Purchase Price	$ 516,813

For your third shop, you will need to borrow $516,813. As before, the bank will first focus on two key measures: your LVR position (that's the total debt to equity ratio of your property portfolio) and your ability to service the loans, which is your interest cover.

For our example, you have been paying the shop loans down with $24,000 of savings per year and $23,060 of positively geared shop income per year, totalling $46,120p.a. of reductions to the combined debt. In addition, each shop has increased in value by 3% per year, further improving your equity position.

When in this position, I had a strong job that paid the bills. I was able to channel all of my savings and positive cashflow into debt reduction on my first shop loan until that loan is paid out, I strongly recommend you also follow that approach if affordable. Then start paying off the second shop loan. From a tax perspective, it makes little difference which loan is paid down because your income tax assessment is derived from total income versus total expenses of your entire portfolio. I suggest paying down one loan at a time as this minimises the number of loans, reducing overall bank fees paid on individual loans.

Remember that, after four years, the total debt against Shop #1 was $105,000. Let's take a look at where it stands after three more years. You have reduced your debt by $72,000 (3 × $24,000) from savings. In addition, the positively geared income from both shops, totalling $69,180 (3 × $23,060), and two years of future rent increments reduce your debt by another $3,600 (2 × $1,800). At the end of Year 7 you will have contributed $144,780 ($72,000 + $69,180 + $3,600) to loan repayments. Your loan on the hairdressing salon is completely paid off, and you have reduced the debt on Shop #2's loan by $39,780 ($144,780 – $105,000).

On Shop #2, you owed $422,268 on which you have been paying only interest to the bank. In Year 7, you pay out Shop #1's loan and begin directing your savings and positive cashflow to Shop #2's loan. Seven years into your wealth-building strategy, you own shop #1 outright and have reduced Shop #2's loan to $382,488.

It's time to focus on Shop #3. The LVR calculation for your three shops would look like this:

$$LVR = \frac{\text{Total Bank Loans}}{\text{Total Property Value}}$$

$$= \frac{\underset{\substack{\text{Shop \#1} \\ 418,055}}{\$0} + \underset{\substack{\text{Shop \#2} \\ 424,360}}{\$382,488} + \underset{\substack{\text{Shop \#3} \\ \$490,000}}{\$516,813}}{}$$

$$= \frac{\$899,301}{\$1,332,415} = \textbf{67.5\%}$$

The LVR is well within the banks' 70/30 target. Taking on the third shop would result in total loans of $899,301, which, on an interest rate of 5%, would cost $44,965 per year. As you would generate a positively geared income from all three shops of $100,600 ($32,023 + $31,827 + $36,750), you would easily cover the 1.5 times income measure, and your loan would be approved.

The following diagram represents your portfolio.

7 YEARS IN

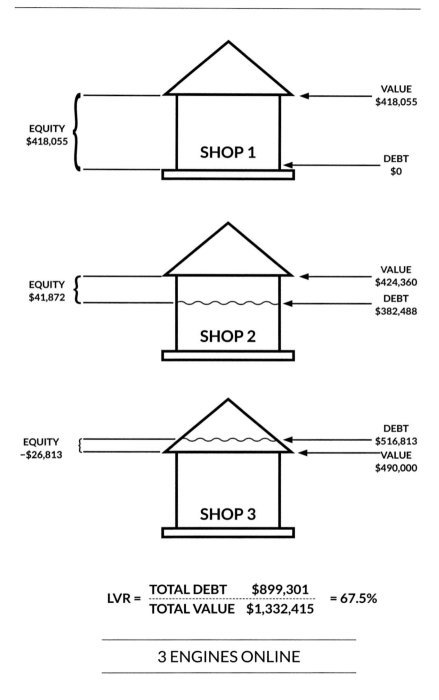

Congratulations! You have three commercial properties or Engines of wealth online and working for you. Let's return to the key ingredient needed to build real, long-lasting wealth — time. While running the shops, you will only need to wait a further two years before your next round of investment because the cumulative power of time is now working its magic on 3 properties!

You have three retail properties generating a combined net rent of $100,600p.a., with an annual interest payment of $44,965. You and your investment partner therefore have a taxable profit of $55,635 ($100,600 - $44,965), which, as before, is calculated as income, requiring you to pay income tax on it. Assuming that you are still in the 30% tax bracket, you will pay $16,691 tax, leaving you with $38,945 per year in after-tax profit to pay down Shop #2's mortgage. Let's put that in perspective, you are generating $750 a week in after-tax profit after just seven years following a low-risk investment strategy.

As you start Year 8 of your retail property investment, wealth-building strategy, you have the following in equity growth: properties valued at $1,332,415 and growing at the conservative assumption of 3% from annual rent increases, which is $39,972 in capital appreciation per year.

Let's add up all of that growing equity:

Combined Savings	$24,000	
Positive Shop Income	$38,945	
Future Rental Increment	$ 2,800	($933 is the average rent increment per year per shop)
Capital Appreciation	$ 39,972	
Equity Growth per annum	**$105,717**	

At this point, you could ask your investment partner, "When was the last time you saved over $105,000 in a year?" The answer for most of us would be "Never!" From now on and every year moving forward, this is what you will add to your net wealth, provided you hold onto this property portfolio.

It's definitely not a "get rich quick" scheme; it has taken you seven years. You have followed a solid investment strategy that leverages savings, positive cashflow and capital appreciation to build real, long-lasting wealth over time. You have three engines of wealth injecting financial support into your life, and the best thing is that the income is indexed to grow above inflation with built-in annual rent increases and market adjustments. At this stage of my journey, I remember saying to my investment partners, "This really is amazing! Imagine what a fourth engine would do to accelerate our finances?" Luckily, they all agreed and we pursued another.

After your first (hypothetical) property, you had to wait four years for Shop #2, then three years more for Shop #3. But, for the fourth property, you only need to wait two years because you are building equity at a much greater rate. In fact, you are building equity at $105,000 per year.

At Year 9 in your investment journey, you have identified another shop to purchase. Your fourth commercial property will cost $520,000 with a net rent of $39,000 at a rate of return of 7.5%. Factoring in bank fees, legal fees and stamp duty, the fourth property has the following purchase profile:

Shop 4 Purchase Price	$ 520,000
Stamp Duty	$ 18,100
Legal Fees	$ 10,000
Total Purchase Price	**$ 548,100**

The first step is to calculate the net rents for the three retail shops purchased previously and their respective property valuations. The table on the following page shows the rents and valuations (growing at 3% per year).

Year	Shop #1 Net Rent	Shop #1 Property Value	Shop #2 Net Rent	Shop #2 Prop. Value	Shop #3 Net Rent	Shop #3 Prop. Value
1	$26,820	$350,000				
2	$27,624	$360,861				
3	$28,453	$371,445				
4	$29,306	$382,592				
5	$30,185	$394,060	$30,000	$400,000		
6	$31,091	$405,882	$30,900	$412,000		
7	$32,023	$418,055	$31,827	$424,360		
8	$32,984	$430,596	$32,782	$437,091	$36,750	$490,000
9	$33,973	$443,514	$33,765	$450,204	$37,852	$504,700

For the fourth time, you visit your bank manager, asking for an investment loan of 100% of the purchase costs, totalling $548,100. By now, you are familiar with the bank's key lending criteria. First, is the LVR. At the end of Year 7, you had two bank loans totalling $899,301. After two more years of saving (2 × $24,000), your positively geared shop income (2 x $38,818), and a future rent increment of $2,800, this debt will have reduced by $128,436. The resulting balance of your loan for Shop #2 is now $254,052 ($382,488 – $128,436). The LVR calculation for four shops looks like this:

$$LVR = \frac{\text{Total Bank Loans}}{\text{Property Value}}$$

$$= \frac{\$0 + \$254,052 + \$516,813 + \$548,100}{\underset{\$443,514}{\text{Shop \#1}} + \underset{\$450,204}{\text{Shop \#2}} + \underset{\$504,700}{\text{Shop \#3}} + \underset{\$520,000}{\text{Shop \#3}}}$$

$$= \frac{\$1,317,165}{\$1,918,418} = \textbf{68.7\%}$$

Although the LVR is higher than last time we visited the bank, it is still within the bank's 70/30 target. Looking at interest cover, taking on the fourth shop would result in total loans of $1,317,165, which, on an interest rate of 5%, would cost $65,858 per year. The positively geared income from all four shops would total $144,590 ($33,973 + $33,765 + $37,852 + 39,000). Like last time, this easily achieves the 1.5 times income measure. Again, the bank clears you for take-off, and you are free to move forward with securing your fourth property.

The diagram on the following page represents the equity mix of your expanding property portfolio:

9 YEARS IN

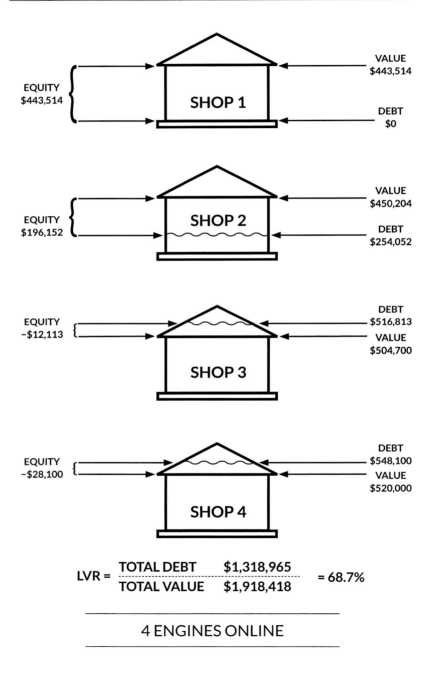

EQUITY
$443,514

SHOP 1

VALUE
$443,514

DEBT
$0

EQUITY
$196,152

SHOP 2

VALUE
$450,204

DEBT
$254,052

EQUITY
–$12,113

SHOP 3

DEBT
$516,813

VALUE
$504,700

EQUITY
–$28,100

SHOP 4

DEBT
$548,100

VALUE
$520,000

$$LVR = \frac{TOTAL\ DEBT \quad \$1,318,965}{TOTAL\ VALUE \quad \$1,918,418} = 68.7\%$$

4 ENGINES ONLINE

After nine years, you and your investment partner enjoy an even greater cashflow position. After your fourth retail property investment, you are left with a taxable profit of ($144,590 - $65,858) = $78,732 per year. Using the 30% tax bracket, you will receive $55,112 per year in after-tax profit, or $1,060 per week.

After adding your 4th property to the portfolio in Year 9, you are generating the following equity each year:

Savings	$ 24,000	
Positive Shop Income	$ 55,112	
Future Rental Increment	$ 3,800	($950 is the average rent increment per year per shop)
Capital Appreciation	$ 95,921	(5% on $1,918,418 worth of property)
Equity Growth per annum	**$178,833**	

In nine years, your property portfolio has established a net equity position of $601,253, it holds $1,918,418 in commercial property and is generating over $178,000 in new equity annually.

One of the very first books I read on investing was titled *Creating Wealth* by Robert G. Allen. It was based on investing in the US residential property market. Allen's strategies, I feel, can also be applied to commercial properties in most countries and economies. For me, one of the key learnings in Allen's book was "The 4 stages of building wealth", which he defined as: Pre-launch, Launch, Pre-Orbit, and Orbit. Robert Allen's wealth-building stages have parallels with the wealth journey defined here:

- Pre-Launch = saving and securing the first deposit
- Launch = purchasing the first commercial property
- Pre-Orbit = getting into an investment rhythm with Shops #2, 3 and 4
- Orbit = securing the fifth property to provide financial freedom

Robert coined the phrase "Orbit", which has stuck with me. In this magical stage of investment, your assets are growing faster than your expenditure each year. Robert declared five properties as his benchmark to achieving "Orbit". With the goal of securing financial orbit, let's stick with the plan and pursue a fifth property.

The waiting period between your investments has been shortening, but, without tipping in extra savings, you will need two years to save sufficient equity to remain below an LVR of 70/30. So, with another two years of equity growth and savings, you start looking for that fifth property. Without going through all of the calculations again, I can confirm that a fifth shop for $550,000 with net rent of $41,250 is possible within an LVR of 70%. The key figures of this portfolio are as follows:

Year 11	Shop #1[5]	Shop #2	Shop #3	Shop #4	Shop #5	Total
Net Rent	$36,042	$35,821	$40,157	$41,375	$41,250	$194,645
Prop. Value	$470,519	$477,617	$535,429	$551,668	$550,000	$2,585,233
Loan Size	$0	$94,028	$516,813	$548,100	$579,300	$1,738,241

After 9 years, your conversation with the bank manager for your fifth property involves an LVR of 67.2%. As with your previous purchases, the interest cover is well under the 1.5 times measure.

At this point, according to Robert G. Allen, you are in "financial orbit". Your annual net rent is $194,645 and the interest on your five shops totals just under $87,000, leaving a post-tax positively geared profit of almost $80,000 per year. After 11 years, your portfolio value now exceeds $2.5 million and has a net equity

---

[5] If you are thinking, why does Shop #2 have a higher value than Shop #1 with a lower net rent? It is because Shop #1 was purchased at a higher Rate of Return, 7.66%, whereas all of the other shops were at 7.5%.

position of almost $847,000. You have achieved all this while keeping your day job and saving a modest amount each month. This is definitely a wealth engine that will keep performing into the future. In fact, it will continue performing long after your death, so you have something quite amazing to leave your children.

When we started this wealth journey and investment example, I reflected on the problem faced by our children today — saving a deposit for a residential house, which turned the traditional Australian Dream of owning your own home into an impossible dream. The strategy outlined here is a stepping stone to wealth for Gen Y (20-30s) and Gen X (40+) who are struggling to secure a deposit for a house. It gets you saving, it gets you into the market, building equity through capital appreciation, and it creates a positively geared income stream that is complemented by savings.

At any time during the 11 years, you could decide to apply your equity and buy your first residential house to live in. If you took on an investment partner, then even after dividing the equity, you have $423,000 at your disposal, with a positively geared income to pay the mortgage. This is more than sufficient for a 20% deposit on a residential property, and a comfortable lifestyle.

As covered in Chapter 2, in Australia your domicile residence is the single most tax-effective investment you can make. The task of saving a deposit is now not a "bridge too far" — you are receiving over $80,000 every year in positively geared income, and that's after tax!

When deciding on a residential purchase, I recommend that you do not sell any of the retail shops — they are a hard-earned equity machine. If you need more equity, wait a year. Once you have your domicile residence, start channelling the positively geared income and savings to pay off your domicile loan, before you pay more off the principle shop loans. The reason for this is that interest on a domicile residential loan is not tax deductable. Also, banks lend at an 80% LVR on residential property, meaning paying this loan down instead of your commercial loans will provide you more borrowing capacity, should you decide to push on and continue expanding your commercial property portfolio.

Regardless of your residential status, the next decision in the context of this long-term wealth strategy is, to use a blackjack phrase, "Hit or Stick?" What will you choose to do in another two years' time — watch your equity grow, or buy another? The next chapter looks at the propagation of wealth through to retirement planning.

For me, I just kept going and, according to my wife, I am too young to stop and retire. I return to my love of Oliver Twist, quoting, "Sir, can I please have some more?"

Chapter 5

PROPAGATE AND SECURE INDEPENDENCE

By now you will understand why I, and many I speak with, agree that retail property investment is the best long-term, wealth-building strategy. Many one-time investors in the market are happy with their investment home or shop, and never progress to the next level. As indicated in Chapter 4, "Riding the Outward Spiral" is all about building a wealth engine with 2, 3, 4 or 5 commercial properties that continue to build wealth, even while you sleep. This chapter continues your journey, taking the hard-earned equity, and reinvesting it into an income stream that can support you long after your death — providing a positive cashflow for your children and grandchildren.

As I consider my pending retirement, wherever that may take me, I ask myself, "How much annual income do I need when I retire?" The answer will be different for everyone. The number you consider today, e.g. $80–100,000, may be sufficient, but in 10, 20 or 30 years, with the escalating cost of living and expensive aged care facilities, it is important to plan on having a little extra money "for a rainy day".

In our example, you achieved an annual income stream of $80,000 per year plus conservative capital growth across your portfolio of $100,000 per year in just 11 years. The question is, "Will this be enough for you?" Let's compare this with Mr and Mrs Normal. I have seen many "normal" people spend their entire working lives paying their mortgage down and, finally, after 30 years, they own their own home. They may also finish with a modest retirement nest egg of superannuation of $300,000 to $500,000. Typically, after 10 years of retirement, this is all gone and they are relegated to living on the government pension. I have one thing to say about the aged care pension, "It is not living; it's surviving". I think it is a brutal existence to end up on the pension because it barely provides enough money to cover the most basic of needs.

I frequently meet successful executives and Managing Directors of small to medium companies who retired after 35 years of service, only to "get bored" or run out of money when they turned 70. I meet these senior Australians driving taxi cabs or Uber. Although I enjoy sharing stories with them, after I retire I am committed to never needing to re-enter the workforce due to money concerns.

Whatever your reasons or motivations, it is reassuring that a wealth strategy like this allows you to "own your decision". That is, as you generate an independent stream of income, you are not a slave to a salary and not at the whim of your boss or company, nor reliant on a pension when you retire. After collecting a retail property portfolio, you can pause, be happy with what you have built, quit your job or keep working, or buy more shops — all are good choices and all totally up to you.

One of the secrets to building long-term wealth is to not rest on your laurels; do not rest contented as many "rainy days" may lie ahead. You could argue that this belief holds an element of greed: the desire to want more, to put your head down and stay committed to what you started, to keep growing your portfolio. Well, yes, it is either greedy or sound, future planning. You may also have philanthropic or community motivations that spur you on to keep growing your portfolio.

As I have stated, I have 51 shops and, yes, I am looking for that next one. I hear people along the way say, "You should be happy with what you've got", and "Money won't make you happy". Without judging, I find those making comments are typically happy with their traditional savings strategy, they never create real wealth, and they live their lives with modest assets. We all have different motivations. Mine is to provide financial and lifestyle security for myself and my family, even after I have passed away. I do not expect the government or my kids to provide financial support when I become fragile and dependent upon others — I feel the need to be self-sustaining.

As explained in Chapter 3, you have built an engine of wealth that provides a consistent and on-going income stream, indexed to grow ahead of inflation each year. You started with a positively geared income stream from one shop, the hairdresser's, which produced a positive income of $196 per week and, while it is a nice bit of extra income, it is certainly not enough to make you rich, especially if you began the investment journey with a 50:50 partner. As highlighted in Chapter 4, if you stick to the game plan and continue expanding your portfolio, you can expect that, with time, like 11 years, your income grows to over $1,500 per week. Using the leverage of equity from many properties, and by growing your portfolio, you will achieve your financial goals, like me, entering orbit and becoming independently wealthy.

The art of investment portfolio propagation and the question as to whether or when you stop expanding the wealth engine is a personal choice. However, I strongly recommend that you only sell your shops when you get an offer that is too good to refuse. After all, when performing, the shops' income grows each year and provides strong security.

I have watched investors buy a property and have that property perform outstandingly, from a tenant and rental perspective and also from a capital growth perspective. After two years, one property was returning an excellent positively geared income and had risen a staggering $120,000 or 40% in value. What happened next, broke my heart. The investor decided he should sell and crystallise his profit. Someone mentioned to him that "it is too good to continue" and, like many in the share market, he felt that he needed to exit before his good fortune was eroded. Sure, there are times when tenants vacate and complain of financial distress (more on this in later chapters). But I always find replacement tenants and, many times, at higher rents than the tenant who left, so I still win. I tell my friends this, "Do not sell a retail shop to realise a short-term gain. This asset class is robust and can withstand market fluctuations more readily than shares. It is a long-term wealth strategy."

I can share that I recently sold a whole centre of shops, seven retail shops in all. I had received an offer too good to refuse. I purchased the centre for $1.65m and generated a good rate of return of 7.2%, increasing annually. The centre was re-zoned by the Council, allowing for residential apartments to be built up to 6 storeys. After owning the centre for twelve years, I was offered $4.2m by a property developer for the whole block — a 254% property increase, or an additional $200,000 per year for every year I had owned it. The profit retired a lot of debt, and it fuelled my purchase of another centre of shops elsewhere.

Consider an investor with a $120,000 equity win. He is viewing the property incorrectly. Yes, the property has a measurable value: he bought it for $300,000 and sold it two years later for $420,000. However, when he sold the shop, the expected profit of $120,000 was eroded. He had to pay capital gains tax because it was an investment, not his domicile residence, and the tax bill was $30,000. Then he put the $90,000 in the bank at 2% interest, securing an interest income of $1,800 per year or $35 per week. I was left scratching my head, thinking that the only thing he achieved by selling his commercial property was to pay the government a lot of tax. He had turned a $120 per week post-tax, positively geared income stream into a $35 per week income stream.

I recommend looking at these properties from an income perspective. Do not reflect on how much profit the property has made by appreciating in value, reflect on the stream of weekly or monthly income the property is contributing to your long-term wealth. The secret to achieving financial freedom is to create an income stream that is indexed to inflation and secured by long-term rental leases.

When you look at investment properties and focus on the annual, positively geared cashflow they generate, I hope this will achieve the following for you:

- Inspire you to keep the properties as they provide a great, positive cashflow. It is the proverbial "goose laying the golden eggs"
- Inspire you to buy another property and keep building this positive cashflow
- Clarify the time when the number of investment shops you own generates enough income to provide you with your desired retirement lifestyle

Some investors "Launch" their wealth engine and, after a few years, get stuck in "Pre-Orbit". That is, after securing 1, 2 or 3 retail shops they, as Robert G. Allen says, "Fail to reach financial orbit". After collecting a few properties and enjoying the positive cashflow each month, there is no doubt that you will start feeling more comfortable about your future. It is at this stage that some become susceptible to kind-hearted friends, or even their wives or husbands, giving advice like:

- Wow, you're so lucky! You should be happy with what you've got
- You shouldn't take on any more debt; you'll risk losing the lot
- You should focus on your family now. You've got enough investments, just be happy
- You are too focused on wealth; money doesn't make you happy
- You've been lucky; don't push your luck
- Borrowing more will just make you a slave to the banks
- I can't believe you'd consider buying another property. Why place yourself under that pressure?
- You might be making money, but you're just creating a job for yourself managing tenants

- It's okay while the interest rates are low, but they won't stay low forever
- Sell! Take the money now and enjoy your life

I have heard all of these comments at dinner parties. My response is the same, "Our choices are our own. I am on a wealth journey beyond my retirement. It has and will take many years. When I'm finished, I will have created financial independence that will provide my family support long after I'm gone." I am an advocate of wanting more. Hence, my predilection for Oliver Twist. I live my life chasing the dream of financial freedom. It is not a crime to own many properties and want more. It is okay to be proud of building a solid financial foundation. Others with differing opinions will always exist — the most important choice is yours.

The key recommendation of this chapter is to stay the course. Remind yourself why you chose retail property investment as your wealth-building engine and keep growing your portfolio. People ask me, "When is a good time to stop?" My answer is, "Wait until you own five properties and ask yourself that question." After you have amassed five properties, you will have achieved a financial orbit where your equity will build much faster than your expenses. I came to the conclusion, "Why not get one more?" Who doesn't like the idea of a little extra cash each month in your retirement?

Factors to consider when answering the question, "When should I stop?":

- When you have achieved a wealthy retirement income or the annual income you desire
- When you are ready to enter retirement
- When you are content with your portfolio
- When you feel your contribution to the family moneybox is complete

For some, like me, we may never stop wanting to expand our portfolios. I actively encourage my children to understand the strategy and to join the movement. It is my hope that, one day, they will retain and manage the portfolio while continuing to propagate it for their children.

The continued propagation over time of your portfolio is essential to growing your income stream for later life — not to survive, but to thrive. For me, a major part of the "Secret Sauce" is not stopping after the first or second shop. It's about pushing on to amass a collection of commercial properties that produces the desired income stream you feel is required for an extraordinary retirement.

Chapter 6

CHARACTERISTICS OF A GREAT RETAIL INVESTMENT

Our focus has been defining retail property investment and clarifying how the economics make it an ideal choice as your long-term wealth engine. Let us fill in the details surrounding property selection and the purchase process. In particular, what should we ask to ensure that we purchase a great shop that leads to a great investment?

- How do you know the shop is in the best location?
- What types of tenants are most attractive?

Best Location

For those familiar with residential property investment, there is one catchcry for determining property value, "LOCATION, LOCATION, LOCATION". For residential property, location may refer to proximity to schools, shops, trains or buses. It may also be about the property's commanding views, access to the beach, a country aspect, or a suburb that is considered more desirable and hence more in demand than other locations. We know that when an area is in high demand, property prices will be at a premium.

For commercial property investment, location is also critical. As a commercial property owner, the one thing I want above all else is a successful, profitable tenant. A tenant who has a successful business is more likely to remain and continue paying rent. Of course, one could argue that if they are too successful they may move on to a bigger, better shop. Such factors are outside of a landlord's control. What we can control, however, is selecting a location that provides tenants with a better chance of success. So, the first consideration when selecting a retail shop is its location.

Given that our target tenants are retailers, they need customers to be successful. The vast majority of tenants rely on high volumes of passing foot traffic to buy their goods and services. Even businesses with a large online internet sales component will typically have a store presence. Location considerations for a retail property investment therefore involve premium access to customers, and lots of them. An attractive retail shop is what I call "in the middle of an ants' nest!". What I mean is that the shop is in a densely populated, residential area, or on a main street, ensuring the tenant has a steady stream of customers walking or driving past their shopfront.

A shop in a well-patronised area means it has access to traffic, ensuring that the property is in high demand by current and prospective business operators. If it becomes vacant, you want strong demand from other tenants to let it, reducing your chance of an extended period of vacancy. A good example is a shop opposite a major train station in the city, or a coffee shop opposite a popular beach. In these two locations, thousands of people walk past the front door daily, providing support for the tenant's business.

Let me expand with a few examples of ideal locations or attributes of a prospective retail shop purchase:

- A doctor's surgery, GP or specialist, located within walking distance of a major hospital
- A café or diner opposite a popular beach
- A shop in a local suburban shopping centre with a proprietary area that won't be built out
- A shop opposite a major train station, school, hospital or government office building
- A shop next door to a post office, major bank, or supermarket
- A shop on the edge of a popular lake or tourist attraction
- A café or takeaway located between several large factories with hundreds of workers nearby

These examples of shop locations have attributes that ensure people are ever present. Note, however, that some may be considered seasonal, like 2 and 6 above. That is, for the warm months of the year, they will be incredibly busy, while, during winter, trade will slow down. In places like Queensland where the coldest months still attract many overseas tourists, trade will be more robust and seasonally resistant. Business locations need a good resource plan to manage the peaks and troughs of stock and staff.

Personally, I like to buy shops in local neighbourhood shopping centres, areas where the council has zoned the land "B2 - Neighbourhood Centre". In most cases, these neighbourhood centres are in mature suburban areas or fully populated housing developments, i.e. these shops are surrounded by swarms of ants. Councils are unlikely to allow a developer to knock down existing housing and re-zone B2 land to build a competing centre nearby, so these neighbourhood centres border on remaining proprietary retail holdings. As part of the council's original community plan, they will most likely remain that suburb's only neighbourhood centre.

In these neighbourhood centres, you will find businesses such as hairdressers, accountants, doctors, pizza shops, Chinese or Italian restaurants, to name a few. Many of these business operators will have operated there for many years, and will be well-known and well-supported by local residents.

Not all locations are equal. Let's take a closer look at what I consider less attractive retail shop locations:

- A shop in a quiet country town with a population of less than 1,000 people
- A shop in a town with no major industry or job prospects
- A shop located on a busy clearway with no parking or ability for customers to stop
- A shop located in a low socio-economic area with high crime rates and signs of graffiti

- A shop dependant on one employer in the town
- A shop located in a seasonal tourist town that only thrives in summer and lies dormant in winter
- A shop in close proximity to a much larger, thriving community shopping centre
- A shop at the back of an arcade with limited visibility

The common concern with these retail properties is that there are simply "not enough ants!" Retail businesses in these quieter areas may struggle to achieve profitability, leading to a higher tenant turnover. Business operators in these quieter areas are more cautious and concerned about their success. Hence, they are less willing to commit to three or five year leases. If not enough people pass by the shop every day, my position is, move on and look for another shop in a better area. The success of your tenant's business is reduced if your property is located in a remote place with a low population, or is in an undesirable area.

Do not be seduced by these properties if offered at higher rates of return, i.e. 8% or 9%, or higher. The risk of a vacancy is high, and the chances of finding a suitable, timely replacement tenant is low.

By now, you may be asking, "How do you find shops in the middle of an ants' nest?" I previously mentioned the source of commercial properties for sale in Australia: *www.realcommercial. com.au*. Enter your search criteria by State, city, price, retail and tenant, and hit enter. You will receive a list of shops for sale to consider. Once I have that list, I go through them, selecting a short-list of desirable candidates for further research.

For the short-list, your first check is the shops location. Go to Google Maps, plug in the address, and select satellite view. You can "virtually" fly over the property, giving you a bird's eye view of the area, including the surrounding neighbourhood, competing shops, and streetscape. Before I zoom in to the candidate, I first zoom out to view the three-kilometre radius around the shop. I make notes on the surrounding area and the number of houses around the shop. Is it in an industrial estate? Is it facing the beach? Does it have a large catchment population who can drive by or walk into the shop? Is the surrounding area densely populated? Is it "in the middle of an ants' nest?"

Once I am satisfied that the shop has the desired location, i.e. it is in a well populated area and has strong consumer traffic, I gain confidence that it will be attractive to tenants and I move forward with my next level of due diligence.

Before moving on from location considerations, I want to answer an often-asked question: "Which Australian State do you prefer investing in?" My answer is that I have no preference for a particular State, only that the investment meets the criteria covered in this book. I currently own retail properties in New South Wales and Queensland. I have, on several occasions, attempted to secure properties in Victoria. However, I've been unsuccessful as they have traded at capitalisation rates well below 6%. So, with buyer demand for Victoria and NSW making it difficult to locate candidates around my target 7.5% return, I place my energy elsewhere.

Another consideration when buying property is the ongoing management of that property. This can lead us to favour properties that are located close to where we live. The thought of driving up the road to fix a problem or talk to a tenant is comforting. Perhaps too, there is vanity in driving by a property that you own. Initially, I held those views, so my first two investments were shops located only 10 minutes' drive from my house. Back then, I bought those properties at excellent capitalisation rates of 8.5% return. Fifteen years on, such deals in NSW are much harder to find.

It was not long into my wealth-building strategy involving retail property that I was forced to expand my horizons and consider other suburbs and, in fact, other States. The ultimate objective is to secure shops in strong locations with tenants able to pay their rent on time. Seeing the shop each day, while a comfort, is not one for which I am willing to pay. My founding investment principle is, "We invest to make money!", for me, that means a target of 7.5% return. The formula covered in earlier chapters: Value = Net Rent / 0.075 was, and remains, my guiding principle. After 10 years of commercial investing in New South Wales, I could no longer find properties at this valuation, so I looked further afield.

My first expansion interstate was into Victoria. To my surprise, I found the market even more heated, with retail shops in and around Melbourne trading at capitalisation rates below 5.5%. For me, investments at 5% to 6% capitalisation pose too much of a risk. A reminder of the economics we shared in Chapter 2: once interest rates start rising and hit 5 or 6%, these investments start losing money unless you have a large nest egg, or capital from an inheritance that you want to turn into a stable, positively geared income stream.

You may be wondering, what about the cost of managing a property located in a different State? At the slightest hint of a problem, you'd need to be on a plane and heading onsite. Wouldn't you? The answer is that I travel to my shops rarely, usually once a year. I found that, after managing my neighbouring properties for over 10 years, I had built up a level of operational control that rarely required my onsite presence. I have expanded on these good property management practices in Chapter 10.

The reason for this apparent "hands off" management style is that the shop tenant is your onsite property manager. Their livelihood that puts food on their table is tied to that shop. Tenants will keep shops tidy for their customers and are responsible for paying for most maintenance, hence they ensure quality maintenance by cleaners and repairers. As mentioned in Chapter 2, most shops are just three brick walls, a glass window, and a concrete floor, so your maintenance is much less than for a residential investment.

"Shop proud" tenants ease the burden of retail shop management, readily allowing for remote ownership. I have found that owning retail property interstate is no more trouble than owning it locally. Thus, I began looking further afield, buying shops in Queensland where valuations were in line with my 7.5% target return.

Queensland is a large State, so your location selection is vital for finding value. Within Brisbane, valuations of sub 7% are becoming the norm. This is a result of greater competition for retail assets from investors, like me, looking north for value. My location focus has therefore moved to other "Ant Nests", like the Gold Coast, Toowoomba, and the ever-growing retirement strip from Coolangatta up to Noosa. Centres like Bundaberg and Townsville offer good rates of return too, however, they are a little isolated and dependent upon specific industries (such as mining and tourism). I suspect that, as the population shifts to find better homes and lifestyles, these locations will become more attractive.

For investors who need to borrow money, a rate of return around 7.5% is where I see value. I encourage others not to get caught up in an over-inflated market, take the emotion out, and move on to the next State. For me, that was Queensland. After that, it might be Western Australia around Perth and, in a few years' time, Tasmania.

Atractive Tenants

The next consideration when procuring a retail property is the existing tenant's commitment or, in other words, the length of the remaining lease. You recall that one of the strengths of investing in shops is that tenants typically sign much longer leases than residential tenants. As a buyer, I look for at least 3–5 years of remaining terms on leases to provide surety of rent.

I once signed a lease to an independent supermarket operator for 25 years. This deal dramatically increased the supermarket's value, improved the value of neighbouring shops, and increased the confidence of my bank in the property.

In many cases, during pre-settlement due diligence (more on this in later chapters), I ask tenants if they would be willing to enter into longer leases, if I bought the building. This approach achieves a couple of things: it confirms the tenant's commitment to the shop and area; and it gives them surety that the new landlord is not going to evict them, which in turn reduces my risk, especially if a tenant has a lease of less than two years to run. I provide tenants with an "Agreement to Lease", which takes effect on settlement. This locks in the tenant and helps with my investment loan discussion with the bank. Remember, banks measure property on WALE (Weighted Average Lease Expiry). If the lease expires in 12 months, banks will be reluctant to provide a fixed or variable loan longer than 12 months. If they do, it will be with conditions and a higher interest rate. A committed tenant with a long lease is therefore critically important to your investment's viability.

During this discussion, a tenant may want something in return for extending their lease, or exercising an available extension option. However, I find this a small price to pay for the security a longer lease provides. Your banker will agree. Things to consider to secure a tenant's agreement include: not applying the 3% or CPI annual rent increase for this year, or lowering the 3% increase to CPI for the term. Reducing the annual rent increase is a good avenue. For tenants, they see this as an immediate saving. For you, as the landlord, you know that when the lease term expires in 3–5 years you will have the opportunity to "market adjust" the rent, restoring your rental position.

Prior to the internet age, you may have believed that all businesses have a place in society, but today, unfortunately, this is not the case. Technology has advanced to the point where the relevance of some businesses is under a spotlight. An obvious example is the traditional video store. With movies being streamed online in homes, DVD rental stores are an endangered species. Only those who have expanded into video games or other areas are surviving. Online gaming however is increasing in its popularity too and will place the final nail in the coffin of the remaining neighbourhood video stores.

Other endangered retailers are newsagents who today live off lottery ticket sales, magazines, and the odd birthday card. Time will not be favourable to these businesses because technology continues to displace these media. Another business on its last legs is traditional, coin-operated laundromats. With improved man-ufacturing techniques dramatically reducing the cost of washers and dryers, these devices are now inexpensive and accessible to all.

Over many years as a landlord, I have developed confidence in certain business types that provide a service or product that is well liked by Australian consumers. The types of businesses operating in your current or potential commercial property are important and can place a premium on the shop's value. For example, a tenant that is part of a national chain will certainly increase the shop's value because the chain and brand provide security over future rental payments. Businesses like The Coffee Club, McDonald's,

Subway, KFC, Red Rooster, Office Works and Woolworths are some examples of successful national chains. It is common that shops with these tenants are signed on long 10–15 year leases and, when up for sale, they secure the seller an attractive rate of return of 5–6%.

Apart from retailers that are national chains, sold at a premium, I have listed on the following pages, in order of preference, various business types I recommend you consider when purchasing commercial property.

Hairdressing Salons

I have six hairdressing salons and I love them as tenants. Everyone needs their hair cut, so this is an essential service. Apart from home stylers and the bald, the demand for hairdressers in any economy is strong, making them almost recession proof. Look for salons that operate in spaces from 40–70m² and have 4–6 cutting stations. Hairdressing salons are easily traded, with many owners selling their business to their staff members when they have had enough. Hence, I rarely have lease vacancies across my six salons. Men and women tend to want their hair cut by the same hairdresser, often the one they have been going to for many years. Customer loyalty is high in this industry, providing exceptional repeat business, which of course means ongoing sustainability.

Over the years, I have sought out well-run hairdressing salons in high foot-traffic areas, which easily support rents from $35,000–$50,000 per year without placing the owner under financial stress. If you are looking to buy a shop with a hairdresser, check if it has been trading for several years, and you will typically find an owner who views the salon as their retirement nest egg, planning to build further value in it and then sell the business to enjoy a slower lifestyle.

For me, hairdressing salons make a great investment.

Bottle Shops

If you want a business that is recession proof, here it is! If the economy is tight, or you're feeling a bit sad, most of us will go to the bottle shop for some "alcoholic cheer". When times are good and we want to celebrate, we will also pick up a few drinks on the way home. The difference is you might spend a bit more in the good times than in the bad. For bottle shops, customers come through the door all year round, no matter what the occasion.

Surveys indicate Australians are among the heavier drinkers in the world, so it is no surprise that many regularly visit the local bottle shop for beer, wine or spirits to celebrate or commiserate.

Bottle shops are also great businesses to add vibrancy to any neighbourhood shopping centre because they attract a lot of consumer traffic. Securing a national chain bottle shop, like Dan Murphy's, BWS, or Bottlemart is a trophy investment property, but any shop or centre with one of these brands will not come cheap. You will pay a premium, but, over the long-term, the strength and stability these businesses offer can't be understated. I keep an eye out for local neighbourhood bottle shops because they make great tenants with a superior ability to pay rent.

Café's

The secret to a good coffee shop is simple: "good coffee served in a nice environment". People will leave their home or office to have a good coffee, so that is a consideration when buying a coffee shop. Of course, the barista has a big part to play in the quality of coffee served, so, unless they are the tenant or business owner, be cautious, as they can be transient and difficult to replace.

The other ingredient for a good coffee shop is ensuring the social factor is high, as primarily drinking coffee is a social thing to do with friends, work colleagues, customers, and family. The old adage "let's catch up for a coffee" is engrained in human behaviour and the workplace. Sharing a cup of coffee is a great way to meet a new client and the medium used to catch up on circulating office gossip. Whether for business or pleasure, good quality barista coffee is always in strong demand.

A café with a view or interesting outlook adds to the ambience of drinking coffee. Looking over the beach, a nice mountain, down the valley, or even a busy city intersection where one can people watch with the chairs arranged side-by-side works well, as mastered by Parisian cafés. Other aspects to consider when targeting coffee shops is any proprietary advantage. For example, being located next to a hospital, school, train station or sporting venue will ensure strong patronage and a vibrant business.

Like bottle shops, coffee shops provide high demand products and national chains like Star Buck's, The Coffee Club, Gloria Jeans, or McDonald's McCafés are solid investments. However, I doubt you will be able to buy these for anything near the target Rate of Return of 7.5%. Typically, they sell in the low 6% range due to their national chain security.

When considering a café, beware of the competition. Setup costs to open a coffee shop are relatively low, and many shopping centres have multiple coffee shops already operating. Regardless of potential alternatives though, demand usually outstrips supply for good coffee and cafés are among the best performers in my portfolio.

Thai, Chinese or Italian Restaurants

Rounding out my top six are my favourite places to eat out with my family. I have six Thai, Chinese, and Italian restaurants across my portfolio and, assuming they are run by astute owner-operated tenants, I find these business types to be gold!

I'm sure you have your favourite Thai, Chinese or Italian restaurant. I admit to being a regular patron at my local Chinese and Thai takeaways. I personally love all three of these restaurant types and have found that, if they offer good food, they are extremely well supported by the community. I have owned a Chinese restaurant for the past 10 years and it has been operating in the same centre since opening in 1984, that's 33 years of constant trading. That rental consistency is why I believe these shops are gold.

I ensure that all shopping centres in my portfolio feature a Thai, Chinese, or Italian Restaurant. I find they have long trading histories, lease ownership stability, and exceptional customer loyalty. I have never experienced a rental vacancy across these restaurants because operators readily sell them to new owners. The three restaurant types cater for dine-in clientele, takeaway, and home deliveries, ensuring that their sales volume is not constrained by seating limitations.

In the same way that a café needs a good barista, when targeting a restaurant, ensure that it serves quality food. Dining in allows you to sample the food, check how busy it gets, and observe the mix of customers. For example, a restaurant that is packed out each night is a good sign of food quality. Another valuable source of research is what other customers think. Scan Google and Trip Advisor for reviews to read feedback on meal quality and service. You can also check Menu Log and Deliveroo takeaway websites for restaurant ratings.

One point to note, however, when buying a restaurant is to ensure that building insurance has been accurately declared in the property's Information Memorandum. Insurance companies will charge you a premium if you are insuring a restaurant compared with insuring a hairdressing salon. In a restaurant, you are cooking and using hot oils. Therefore, it presents a greater fire risk for insurers.

In my opinion, I think it's hard to go wrong with buying a Chinese, Thai, or Italian Restaurant that is well supported, has good food, and has been operated for many years. My personal experience as an owner and consumer shows that demand for takeaway food increases each year.

I cannot separate these three restaurants in my Top 6. I believe that, as prospective tenants, they are all equally gold.

Pizza Shops

I separate pizza shops from Italian restaurants as it is a different business model. Pizza shops can have a very limited eat-in capacity, in some cases less than five tables. The secret to their success is strong home deliveries and takeaway. I have two Pizza shops that both trade strongly. The pizza business is well supported by Australians and home-delivered pizza is almost a staple "night off from cooking" past-time.

Many pizza franchises operate today, including Pizza Hut, Dominos, Crust, Pizza Temptations, and Pizza Capers, to name a few. Securing one of these larger brands is better than a smaller, less well recognised business, but, as mentioned earlier, chain security generally means a lower Rate of Return.

The sign of a good pizza shop is the vibrancy of the store and the number of staff and delivery drivers who work each night. Location too is important for this business type, selecting a suburb with a younger demographic and a higher proportion of dual-income families means that more people are eating out. Sydney's north shore, Melbourne's inner east, and Perth's Mount Lawley are locations where a good pizza shop can do well, even with nearby competing pizza outlets.

When targeting a pizza shop, ensure you eat-in and watch how many customers come through the doors. Some shops will have liquor licences, and this adds strength to the business as it attracts more in-store diners.

I like pizza shops as they make a stable investment option, but it does come down to a successful operator. With plenty of competition around, experience, a good menu, and strong location are key.

Accountants

Over the past seven years, I have had four accountant tenants, all of whom occupied upstairs office space, not ground-floor retail space. I do not target accountants when I look to purchase a shopping centre with 5–12 shops. They typically are part of the mix and occupy the upstairs offices, which are not attractive to most retailers due to the lack of passing foot traffic and limited retail exposure.

I do find, however, that accountancy practices are a solid business type, adding value to larger shopping centre investments. These businesses are similar to bottle shops in that they are recession proof. Most of the working population and all companies must submit annual tax returns, and, with taxation policy getting more complex, accountants are more in demand.

Most tax payers use the same accountant every year because they know your history, they know what tax deductions you have made, and, to be honest, it is just easier to look to the same professional to resolve one of those dreaded annual rituals (up there with the dentist). That trust and longevity make them an attractive tenant. They rarely move and they occupy upstairs floor space that most retailers do not want. I personally have had the same accountant my entire life and he has been in the same upstairs office space for over 30 years.

Accountants who start on the ground floor to establish their business and brand will typically move to less expensive upstairs office space because they usually do not rely on passing traffic and high exposure to build their client base. Accountants capture new customers through word-of-mouth recommendations, sponsoring local sports clubs, and advertising in local papers. If you are buying a retail building that has an upstairs office with an established accountant then that's gold!

If, however, you are buying a street frontage retail shop with an accountant as the tenant, I would be cautious on the level of rent being paid. I would need to be comfortable with the location and the shop's relevance to other business types at that rent level, in case the accountant leaves for a lower, upstairs rent position.

Law Firms

Law firms have many similarities with accountancy firms. They do not require high exposure, ground floor retail space. I manage shops with two law firms and both are in upstairs office space.

Lawyers specialise in various legal fields, including family law, estate law, or conveyancing, to name a few. With the property market being so buoyant over the past ten years, business for conveyance lawyers has been steady, making them attractive tenants. Conveyancing lawyers are another recession proof business. Families are always upgrading or downsizing their homes, so it is fair to say that conveyancers are a well-supported business type with a proprietary need in our community.

Estate law is another area that I find has a well-supported customer base. Many people seek out the support of a lawyer to put a Will and estate management plan in place. For this reason, Estate Lawyers will continue to be well supported business types.

Probably the most common legal specialisation is family law, driven by the increasing number of divorces. Every day in Australia, while 300 couples marry, 128 couples get divorced[6]! Of those divorces, 47% involve children, making those divorces that little bit more emotional and complex. It's fair to say that the demand for family law services will not decline, making them attractive tenants in your shop.

My opinion of various legal professions is irrelevant when it comes to what makes an attractive tenant who pays their rent on time. I have found that lawyers make excellent tenants as their businesses are in demand by the community and because they charge rates that are a premium to other professional service businesses.

Doctors, Pathologists, Optometrists, Laser Clinics, Physiotherapists and Medical Services

I have grouped these medical professionals together because they cross-refer, and the dynamics of their businesses are similar. I have several of these business types operating in my centres and they are among some of the best businesses types as tenants. They rarely have difficulty in paying rent, and they tend to stay in one location for extended periods.

Doctors are another recession proof business. When you or your kids are sick, you take them to the local GP or, if serious, the hospital. Again, like accountancy services, loyalty draws customers to return as your chosen GP knows your medical history, and you build trust over time. In addition, they understand your family's conditions, anxieties, and background. Doctors establish a strong customer base that will often stay with them across generations, making them attractive tenants.

---

[6] Australian Bureau of Statistics 2016.

Pathology centres also make good tenants with a captive market as doctors cross-refer when they want confirmation via blood tests. Their patients are generally older, serving those who need to have their blood tested regularly. Pathology centres provide a critical service to the community and are hence well supported.

Optometrists provide services that are also in high demand. With an aging population, the demand for glasses, contact lenses, or corrective surgery is increasing. Add to that replacement pairs of glasses when they are scratched, broken or simply lost, and that means a constant demand for optometrists. Securing an optometrist as a tenant in your retail shop will increase its value and offer great rental security.

Doctors, pathologists, optometrists, laser clinics, and physiotherapists are solid tenants. However, they have one escalating downside — insurance premiums. Increasing regulations for higher professional indemnity insurance, occupational safety, and other requirements makes it difficult for GPs and others to run a profitable practice on their own. They look for two or more practitioners to partner with and run a clinic, sharing the growing insurance burden.

For practitioners in alternative medicines, including acupuncture, homeopathy, various forms of massage, aromatherapy, and others, while they provide a valuable service to many, greater forces make them less attractive as tenants. Australian government policy has discouraged consumers from these alternative providers by removing them from the approved list of health insurance providers. Consequently, patients are unable to claim rebates on treatments by these alternative providers. Although I personally feel that these providers deliver a valuable community service, without government support, they struggle.

Vet Clinics

I have had only one vet clinic, and that tenant remained with me for well over 14 years before I sold the building. We know the expression that "a dog is a man's best friend", well, like kids, I found the family pet gets equal attention when something goes wrong. With demand for pets growing, I rate vet clinics highly, alongside doctor surgeries, as favourable tenants.

A friend of mine spent $200 on vet bills to heal her injured chicken. You can buy a chicken for around $20, so this demonstrates the expense people are willing to go to for their much loved pets. I watch a TV series called *Bondi Vet* and I regularly see people spending thousands on cancer treatments and bone reconstructions for their injured animals.

Last month, my dog was lethargic and my wife instantly raced him to the vet. I made a comment that he'd probably just eaten a frog and needed to sleep it off. She replied, "I don't pay vet insurance to take the risk that he'll sleep it off." This growing trend of insuring cats and dogs has ensured a constant flow of business for vets from an ever-growing community of pet lovers.

Bakeries

I have two bakeries and have found them to be solid businesses, which increase the vibrancy through constant foot traffic within a shopping centre. Astute bakers have evolved their offerings past loaves and rolls, to cater for lunchtime meat pies and sausage roll-eating tradesmen, to vanilla slice or coffee cake treats for shopping mothers, and pizza and vegemite rolls for after-school kid treats.

I have found that good bakeries are well supported by locals, and consider bakeries as suitable tenants with an excellent ability to pay their rent, if run well. Like coffee and pizza shops, securing a national brand like Brumby's or Baker's Delight adds value to your retail investment. Other related cake eateries are good investments too, if you target national chains, such as Muffin Break, Dunkin' Donuts or Krispy Kreme. Specialty or independent cake shops, such as wedding cake bakers, have their place, but are not high on my list of target tenants.

Real Estate Agents

Over the years, I have been able to add L J Hooker and Ray White real estate agents to my portfolio. They are all franchise stores with a local principal. They are in my top tenants list, with success underpinned by having a strong rent role to generate a continuous revenue stream. A good real estate agency needs to have about 100 properties under management to keep the lights on and pay the bills, while they chase lucrative commissions from property sales.

The Australian real estate market has been strong over the past seven years with property prices sharply rising across most States, leading to strong property turnover and commissions. In the past year or so, these higher prices have caused the supply of properties for sale to slow down, low supply means fewer homes to sell, and real estate agents are competing harder for listings and trimming their commission. Overheated house prices or stagnant economies mean lower turnover, reduced profits, and pressure on businesses without a strong rent book.

Another factor emerging through the wider adoption of internet advertising is an increasing number of "web presence only" agencies who offer flat-rate 1% commission deals. Online agencies are taking a bite out of this industry, and it is fair to say that this pressure will continue.

Massage Centres

I own one Thai massage centre in my portfolio and always find it is busy and well booked. Massage centres can be boom or bust, given they have low setup costs. When targeting a shop with this tenant you need to consider their investment and experience. They must be in a busy area, not in a backstreet, the fit-out needs to be stylish, not cheap or tacky, and it must be big enough for at least 3-4 separate rooms because volume is necessary to provide business security. There are a few national chains (Golden Door and Endota Spa) which tend to have long leases and are good investments.

I use a massage centre regularly to treat back soreness. However, for many, a massage is considered a luxury and only affordable as a treat. Massage centres do well from gift vouchers from husbands not knowing what to get their wife for their birthday. I have had my massage tenant for six years. It is a strong, popular business which invested in an expensive, stylish fit-out and who always pays the rent on time. I rate these businesses as attractive, but recognise that many in this industry are not good investments.

Supermarkets

I round-out my attractive tenant list with tenants who I consider the "mother-load". Supermarkets are high income, large floor space, and generally on long leases, 15+ year tenants. With most being national brands (Woolworths, Coles, IGA, FoodWorks, Night Owl, Spar, Friendly Grocer), they come with large price tags and low Rates of Return, below 5.5%.

Although I love a challenge, these shops and tenants are usually priced out of my reach. If you have the few million required for one of these stores, they offer incredible security with 20-year leases not uncommon. Unfortunately, due to the outstanding security of rent from a triple A-rated tenant, you can expect to pay premium prices for these assets. If you have excess capital and want to turn this into long-term income, supermarkets are a great investment.

For me, I believe interest rates will return to 5-6% one day and, if you borrow the money for this shop, you may lose money. My valuation target is based on a 7.5% return and, while I would consider lower returns to secure top quality premium assets such as a Woolworths or Coles, buying below 6.5% is my floor, after which the risk of loss through rising interest rates becomes too great.

Having said that, I do have three convenience stores as anchor tenants in separate neighbourhood shopping centres: I find these two IGAs and one FoodWorks to be excellent tenants with strong turnovers, fuelled by regular, local clientele. I reserve the term "super" market for Coles, Aldi, and Woolworths stores. Convenience centres serve the surrounding suburb of customers who call in for odd items, like bread, milk, cheese, bacon, or maybe a magazine. Customers tend to do their big weekly or fortnightly shop at larger supermarkets. IGA, FoodWorks, Spar and Night Owl stores are examples of smaller convenience centres, and I have found these tenants extremely reliable and rate them in the gold category.

Less Attractive Business Types

The 15 most attractive tenants are listed above, in my priority order. The six tenants that I will not target and who would potentially cause me to walk away from a sale are listed on the following pages. Typically, these less desirable tenants have an unsustainable business model, leading to rent defaults and shop closures, resulting in vacancies and rent loss for the landlord. The other concern is the pressure these operators place on landlords to reduce the rent in order for them to survive and continue operating their failing businesses.

Video Shops

If there is a video store still in operation, I consider them "The Walking Dead". The boom years of the VCR and Video Shop of the 1980s and 90s have been replaced by digital and internet alternatives. Foxtel and AUSTAR took a large bite out of this industry, but the recent introduction of Stan, Netflix and Apple TV have made the traditional video store defunct. The hassle of picking up a video and returning it the next day is gone — every title is available online, all the time.

There is a trend for new release movie DVDs to be dispensed from kiosks, like a vending machine selling Coke. These vending machines are in train stations and shopping centres in lower socio-economic areas, targeting consumers not willing to pay for a Foxtel subscription.

If you are considering buying a retail shop that has a video store as its tenant, I suggest that you think again or maybe consider what other tenants could be suitable for that location, as it will only be a matter of time before you need to find a new tenant.

Newsagents

You may consider a newsagent as an important shop within the dynamic of a neighbourhood shopping centre as they bring in foot traffic. Why then are they on my unwanted list, you may ask? The majority of their traffic is buying lottery tickets or a newspaper. 20% of a newsagents' floor space generates 90% of their profit — the traditional racks of newspapers, birthday cards and magazines are a dying business.

I love spending 30 minutes browsing magazines and newspapers in a newsagent when I'm killing time at an airport, but I get most of my news and current affairs online via websites through my phone or computer. Once the Australian public warms to buying lottery tickets online, or savvy sellers install European-style lottery booths on busy streets, the newsagents' profit engine will evaporate. I do not have any newsagents in my portfolio and, to be honest, have not had any operators knocking on my door to open a newsagency.

I can only assume that those operators managing to pay their rent are not interested in expanding to other locations. I certainly fear for their future and would avoid placing a high value on any shop with this business type as its key tenant.

Laundromats

Like video stores, laundromats were quite popular in the 1970s and 1980s. Most laundromats today are located in lower so-cio-economic areas or backpacker/tourist communities. I still see the odd laundromat in areas of high density living, but, unless they service hotels and restaurants needing regular laundry services, the consumer market has long opted for the convenience and hygiene of their own washing machine.

TABs

Here is one you might find a surprise on the endangered list, TAB offices. A national chain operation such as the TAB, supported by millions of punters every weekend, not to mention the crazed gambling that occurs during major sporting events like the Melbourne Cup, Oak's Day, the NRL and AFL series. You name it and odds are someone has a TAB bet on it.

So why are TABs on my no buy list? Gambling is thriving, however, this business is undergoing dramatic technology change in how it connects with its customers. With the advent of smart phones and secure mobile technology, online gaming sites can now ramp up gaming capacity from hundreds to millions, leveraging cloud-based technology providers. New technologies allow massive scale-up capacity for peak workloads, like the Melbourne Cup, the Australian Open, or the NRL Grand Final.

No longer does a customer need to make their way to a smelly, old-fashioned TAB outlet to place their bet; no longer do they need to wait to collect their winnings. Bets can be placed on a smart phone betting app, or other internet-based apps. The need for TABs to maintain an expensive retail store location is over and many are being phased out across the country.

Specialty Stores

These stores are not exactly mainstream business types. You may recognise them as crystal or rock shops, Two Dollar shops, tarot card readers or spiritual shops, Home Brewing shops, small book stores, gift shops, and boutique homeware stores.

I have found these types of stores rarely last to the end of a lease and rarely extend for a further term. In some cases, these businesses do survive but seldom thrive. Many begin well, but after a while the clientele lose interest or have no need to regularly visit. Within this list, I have found that homewares businesses can work well if the tenant is savvy and imports Asian furniture and household items. However, as the successful ones grow, they typically look for larger warehouse-style locations, leaving you to find another tenant.

As a general rule, I find that these specialty business types struggle to consistently make the rent and invariably approach you, the landlord, for a rent reduction, before ultimately leaving.

Indian Restaurants

You may be surprised to see this seemingly popular Australian dining option on my unwanted list. My experience with Indian takeaway operators is the reason I avoid them as tenants. I have owned several Indian restaurants over the years and all of them have failed to complete the lease and make the business viable. Each restaurant was within a shopping centre that was well populated and was next to a successful Thai, Chinese or Italian restaurant, so I could find no reason why the Indian restaurants should not also be successful. My belief is a lack of experience and business acumen of the particular operators in those situations resulted in continued failures.

I have also formed the view that Indian restaurants are simply not as popular with Australian diners as Italian, Thai or Chinese restaurants. Ask yourself the question "Do you regularly go out to an Indian restaurant for dinner?"

As a result, I only purchase shops with these tenants at higher rates of return and only if the shop is well-located or can be readily let to another business if it becomes vacant.

Whether you are looking to buy independent shops or a shopping centre with five or more retailers, the experiences above will help guide you to the most attractive investment. My top tips for selecting a great shop investment are these:

1. Location: find a shop in an ants' nest; there is no such thing as having too many customers
2. Look for shops with businesses that provide essential services, such as hairdressers, dentists, doctors, or bottle shops
3. Determine if the tenants have been in business for 10 years or longer, in this location or another

4. Look for complementary businesses that drive greater foot traffic. Cafés next to gyms, Italian restaurants beside movie theatres, or bakeries near supermarkets are ideal

5. Understand if they are owner-occupied. A successful business often comes down to the passion, consumer-focus, and drive injected by the tenant. When tenants own and operate the business, his or her personal wealth is tied to its success, giving you a greater chance for success

6. Don't compromise on quality. Consider properties in other States and seek the returns you want with tenants you have confidence in.

A good retail property investment is a combination of many factors and you need to look for investments that tick all boxes in these areas. As you build your knowledge, it is good to engage with other property investors, they love to talk about their latest investment. My advice is to strike up conversations with other commercial investors and learn from their experiences with different business types. We are never too old to learn, so always keep building your knowledge around successful businesses and locations.

Chapter 7

FINDING YOUR COMMERCIAL PROPERTY

Refining the critical steps and techniques to secure a commercial property is a skill that I have been honing for 20 years, and I'm still learning. Like any property purchase, before you turn up to an auction or begin negotiating, you must understand your budget and limits. We all have our limits and need to ensure we stay within them to avoid becoming exposed financially. Whether you are a 20-year-old in your first job starting out or over 50 with equity in your home, the principle is the same, only the borrowing limit varies. Your financial situation will dictate the size of your first shop investment.

In Chapter 3, we looked at techniques to save your first deposit to get started, now it's time to outline the key steps in closing the deal on your target property. The process involves undertaking desk research and communicating with the tenant and agent to improve your negotiating position and maximise your rate of return.

The good news is that the commercial retail market can cater for all the different types of investor budgets, so whether you are looking for a small, entry-level investment, below $400,000, a medium-sized investment of $600,000 to $800,000, or a significant investment of $2-$5 million, something will be available for you. If you have a very large financial appetite, bigger fish are out there. I regularly see 10–15 shops in a shopping centre for sale, or the odd Bunnings store that sells in the $30-$50 million range. I take inspiration from these listings, imagining myself with pockets that deep one day. Who knows? As long as I stay on course with my wealth-building strategy, I may have a financial engine big enough to consume a catch that size one day.

Recapping on the calculations in Chapter 3, you should have a spending limit in mind and a rate of return that suits your budget. Let us assume that you have saved $200,000 either in a share portfolio or by building equity in your home. With this deposit, we can work backwards to estimate the net rent of a shop that will fit your investment budget. This budget allows you to adjust your online property searches (realcommercial.com.au) to display only those properties that fit within your spending limit.

Determining your spending limit uses the LVR (Loan to Value Ratio) from earlier chapters (this determines what the bank is willing to lend). As a first-time lender, the bank will probably request from you a 65/35 LVR position. You could shop around for another bank lending at 70/30 if required, but, for our example, we will assume you accept the 65/35 LVR and contribute 35% of the property's value. The formula is as follows:

Borrowing Capacity = Equity / 0.35

With the $200,000 available, you are able to spend $200,000/0.35 = $571,428.

Remember, we need to factor in the costs of purchase that the bank will not fund, i.e. stamp duty and legal fees. A retail property in Queensland valued at $540,000 will draw stamp duty of $20,000 and, with legal and other bank fees around $10,000, these will lower your borrowing limit. A total borrowing capacity of $570,000 means properties up to a maximum value of $540,000 are within your price range.

Property Budget Limit = Borrowing Capacity – Purchase Costs

Some commercial property listings will state an asking price. However, this is not the norm. One of the more common forms of listing will simply state the property's net rent position. Most agents will offer you what is called an Information Memorandum or IM Pack, which details the property's gross rent and total expenses, and highlights the net rent position. Before you start the process of finding a candidate shop, you should therefore calculate a net rent position that fits within your $540,000 budget.

By knowing what net rent position is acceptable to you, you can quickly determine if a commercial property is within your budget.

In Chapter 2, we enacted the valuation method that has guided the commercial property market over the past few decades:

$$\text{Value} = \frac{\text{Net Rent}}{0.075 \text{ (our target 7.5\% return)}}$$

We can re-write this as: Net Rent = Value × 0.075

You can calculate then that your $540,000 limit for a shop results in an ideal net rent position of $540,000 x 0.075 = $40,500 per year. Armed with a spending limit and a net rent position, you will optimise the process of searching and prioritising shops that are worthy of detailed research.

Let the hunt begin! We have indicated that the best source of shops for sale is the internet, but let's reflect on another, the weekend newspaper property lift-out. Twenty years ago, all property for sale was listed in the paper. Today, this is the domain for residential sales in the local area. Commercial properties are predominantly advertised online, allowing interstate buyers to search for location, price, and other criteria more efficiently.

The best sources to search for commercial property for sale are the following websites:

1) Realcommercial.com
2) Commercialrealestate.com
3) Commercialview.com

These sites contain search filters that allow you to specify criteria to match your needs:

- Select States (WA, QLD) or suburbs (Perth CBD, Noosa)
- Commercial property types – Retail, Office, Medical, Factory, Warehouse

- Key words, such as "Shopping Centre", "Neighbourhood Centre", "Strata Shop"
- Business types, such as "Hair Dresser", "Bottle Shop", "Doctor"
- And, of course, the most important filter, set your minimum and maximum price.

One search criterion available on these sites that is worthy of greater discussion is for those buyers who want a retailer to be the owner/occupier, that is the landlord and the tenant. The first filter check box on these sites is to: Buy, Lease, or Invest. For an owner/ occupier, you want to select "Buy" and include in the key word filter, "Vacant" possession. A word of warning for investors: if you purchase a vacant shop, it is not deemed by the Australian Tax Office to be a "going concern" and therefore GST of 10% applies to the sale. My advice, if you are an investor, is to only search for a tenanted property.

To give you a sense of the scale of investments available at any time, I just went into *www.realcommercial.com.au* and ran an open search for all "Retail Property" to "Buy" in Queensland. The result was 1,522 listings. To review, discarding and prioritising this many listings would take many hours and lots of effort to produce a shortlist of 10–15 shops for detailed research. I have sat down with a cold beer on a Sunday and done exactly that, looking through every advertisement. It took me five hours to scan every property on the Queensland market. This is quick, considering I know what property types I want and could quickly discard those not fitting my criteria.

Although this is a useful exercise for first-time investors to understand what is on the market, it is tedious. For this reason, I would plug into your search filters key words, specific areas, and maximum price ranges, to cut that list back. Selecting an area, like the Gold Coast, Brisbane CBD, or Bundaberg, will reduce the list of candidates to less than 200: a more manageable list, and one likely to result in five or more potential shops worthy of investigation.

Using our example investment of $540,000, I plugged in Queensland retail properties to Buy, and set the maximum price to $540,000. My search returned 658 properties for sale, which is still a lot of properties. By refining the search to Brisbane CBD and the Gold Coast, I identified 312 properties. The reason for selecting this area is, if you live interstate or even if you are a Brisbane local, it is easy to fly in or drive for a reconnaissance trip. Before you make a serious offer to buy one or more of the candidates, visiting the property is vital. We will outline later what to look for, but the objective is to have a selection of shops that are within a few hours' drive.

My colleague, Stephen (the over-50, late bloomer to retail investing, mentioned in Chapter 3), did exactly this to secure his first commercial property. Stephen diligently reviewed the ads for 440 properties on sale in the 250km strip from the Gold Coast to Noosa, prioritising just eight. He then scheduled a weekend road trip, informed the respective agents that he was coming, arranged to see the tenants, and spent an hour onsite before moving on to the next candidate. This "road trip" process is critical to select the 1, 2 or 3 properties that you want to pursue with an offer.

What do you look for when confronted with a few hundred potential properties to buy? You start at the top of the list and work your way down. The website listing provides a short heading, usually the price or address, a small picture of the shopfront, what the net rent position is, and a button to view more detail. Greater detail will expand on another webpage link with 3–5 photos, details on the tenant, the length of the lease, square metre size of the shop, strata or freestanding building, the tenant's business type, and other sales details.

Based on what you learned in Chapter 6, you can de-prioritise properties with less attractive tenants. Other things to look for to eliminate candidates include:

- Does the building look old or run down? Is it a new strata construction (these properties provide great depreciation schedules for your tax return)
- Is it in an area that you know is well patronised, i.e. heavy foot traffic, Ants' Nest?
- Does the sale price and net rent match your target 7.5% return? That is, if the shop's asking price is $500,000, but the net rent is only $30,000, then this would be a 6% return and potentially too expensive. You may be able to negotiate a price of $400,000 (7.5%), but if any of the other criteria above are sub-optimal, this could be a reason to discard this property
- Is it tenanted with a short lease, i.e. less than 2 years? Banks may resist providing a loan for a shop with a short-term lease. If the shop is vacant, it may be attractive for an owner-occupier, but, as it is not a "Going Concern", as mentioned earlier, an investor will pay GST, adding a further 10% to the price tag. In addition, you will be left with the challenge of finding a suitable tenant and will incur a period of vacancy. You may even need to offer a fit-out contribution or "rent free period" to the incoming tenant.

When you view the shop's details, remember that the real estate agent wrote these notes to encourage you to buy the shop, so remain critical of everything you read.

You may ask, "How do I know if an area is attractive, affluent, or well patronised?" You may never have heard of let alone visited many locations on the list. This requires my next most visited website, Google Earth. Plug the shop's address into

Google Earth and take a look at the property and surrounding area. This technology gives you, the buyer, power to quickly look at the location, proximity to beaches, schools, trains, etc. This knowledge is absolutely invaluable, and will save you time driving around to unattractive candidates.

Google Earth allows you to zoom out to approximately three kilometres above a property. From there, I am looking for one thing only, a densely-populated area. Remember one of our rules: "Is the property in the middle of an ants' nest?" Lots of houses around a property means plenty of customers available to support the shop's business.

Once I am satisfied that the area is well populated, I scan around, taking notes on particular features of the area: such as nearby schools, train stations, hospital, beaches, waterways, large government buildings, or anything that could provide a steady stream of customers. Another thing to be wary of is competition: Google Maps highlights nearby restaurants and cafés. Is the shop opposite a shopping centre? Perhaps there is a Westfield Shopping Centre or Coles supermarket up the road.

Your objective is to quickly determine the shop's attractiveness for deeper research. After taking note of what is nearby, I zoom in on the property and enter Street View. This is where Google Earth's technology is incredible for a property buyer. I can virtually walk around the street, check out if the shops in the street are vacant or for lease, see the quality of the street front and environment, and even count how many people and cars are on the street. The technology is so clear that you can zoom in on neighbouring shopfronts and read their telephone numbers off the building. Yes, I have been known to call those tenants and ask them, "How's business?"

If the location, street, neighbours, and other factors are positive and you want to prioritise this shop, a button on the website can send the agent an email. When you select this, it requests your name, email and mobile number. A selection box requests your status: Are you an investor or business owner? The most important is the check boxes underneath, the relevant ones are:

1) Give me an indication of price
2) Notify me about similar properties
3) Send me the IM Pack

The IM pack is the Information Memorandum, which contains 10–15 pages detailing the property and sometimes the tenant. This is the agent's selling document, so again be mindful that, although all statements must be accurate, they are written in the seller's favour. I always click all three check boxes because agents often have "off market" listings or listings they know are coming up, but as yet are not on their books or listed on the internet.

By this time, you will have a high opinion of the property and should have a feeling that it is worth pursuing. If so, make a note of the property's address, write down the agent's phone number (as they always call to follow up), then wait for the IM Pack to arrive. It usually takes a few hours, if it takes longer then the agent may not have the IM ready (sometimes they list the shop to determine the level of interest, ahead of the seller investing in the IM sales document).

Once you have taken note of the property tab, return to your list and keep searching. I recommend you build a short-list of about 10 properties that you follow-up and request the IM pack on. I expect to whittle this down to a list of five candidates who are worthy of the next level of scrutiny: meeting with the agent and conducting a site visit.

Ultimately, you are looking for an owner who wants to sell the building more than you want to buy it. You will come across owners who are not in a hurry to sell and have unrealistic expectations about what their property is worth. I regularly see owners asking for capitalisation rates of return around 5 or 6%. Because some buyers are prepared to pay at that level, it attracts other owners who list their properties, expecting to get the same return. Like any property purchase, do not get caught up in that "sales madness" and remember, with bank interest rates around 4–5%, I see value at 7.5%. You are not going to live in the shop. The only reason you buy retail shops is to make money, so keep that in mind and move on when price expectations are too high. That is why you have a short-list of several properties.

The Information Memoranda start arriving in your inbox. They all have roughly the same format and content. Typically, the cover shows a great photo or air-brushed picture of the shop and a fantastic write up that extolls the virtues of the surrounding area, traffic flow, and expected population growth. In some cases, the IM Pack highlights future Council spending or major, planned works. This is all designed to get you excited about the potential capital growth of the shop.

Let's focus on the important facts that you need to collect from the IM pack to build your knowledge and determine its attractiveness versus the other properties you are researching. Note, you should also create a list of questions for the agent, so have your pen and paper ready. The following information is listed in priority order for the buyer:

Term of the Lease

This is the most important aspect for you and the bank. The longer the remaining lease term, the more security you have over future rental income. Common terms are 3, 5, and 7-year terms.

Occasionally, you may see 10, 15 and 20-year leases, but these lengths are typically for national chain tenants in large shopping centres, service stations, and supermarkets.

A tenant with a lease term of only 12 months can be a sign of weakness in the investment or the tenant. It could mean that the tenant has recently started the business and has not yet built up the confidence to commit long term. In some cases, tenants may be elderly and thinking of retirement, and hence do not want to commit long term. Either way, I see short, 12-month leases as a negative — the business will be the tenant's livelihood, so any tenant not wanting to lock this in for 3–5 years isn't sending us the right signal about the strength of their business.

A shop with a remaining lease term of 1 or 2 years highlights a risk and opportunity. The risk is the tenant may not stay and the bank will be nervous that the rent is not secured to support the loan. The opportunity is that, if the tenant is under-paying, there is rent increase potential in the shop with a new tenant. On some occasions, the tenant may not be right for the area and, given the location and potential of the shop, you may do better with another tenant. I have had numerous situations where I have inserted a new tenant in a shop on a higher rent, sometimes 15–20% higher.

Although the potential for rental increases is an attractive upside and boosts your rate of return, the preference is a long lease with a tenant committed to growing their business in that neighbourhood.

Length of Lease Options

My view of lease options is that they are there for the tenant's benefit, not the landlord's. They offer the landlord no security or tenant commitment. Options simply provide the tenant the right to continue renting the shop under the exact terms and conditions of the existing lease for a further period after lease expiry. The tenant can always leave and not exercise their option. So, I don't add any value to option periods. For the landlord, it reduces your flexibility to change tenants and improve the mix if you have more than one shop in a centre.

The common lease extension options are: 1 × 3 years, 2 × 3 years, 1 × 5 years. I occasionally come across 4 × 5 year options on leases, which means that, for the next 20 years, your tenant has the power to remain in the premises. If, 10 years later, the council rezones the site for multi-storey development or the site is already approved for development, then this potential development value is locked up until the entire lease term has expired. You may need to wait 20 years before you can develop the site and release its capital value.

So, why even give the tenant an option, you might ask? Some tenants, when entering a lease, demand option periods because they want to be sure they have the right to occupy the building well into the future. Some invest a lot of money in fitting out their shop. A restaurant may need an expensive kitchen fit-out that can cost upwards of $200,000, an IGA requires a lot of space and some fit-outs can run over the $500,000 mark, so lease terms of up to 20 years are requested to ensure their tenure is long enough to recoup these fit-out costs.

One reason landlords like an option is that, upon the tenant exercising the option term, it is less expensive than having a solicitor draft up an entirely new lease. Another advantage to the landlord in providing the tenant an option is that the lease can specify a notice period for renewal. For example, in the lease you can state, "The tenant must exercise their option six months prior to lease expiry". In doing this, you have plenty of notice to advertise and secure a new tenant if they do not renew their lease.

Gross Rent

The IM Pack will detail the total rent payable by the tenant under the lease. The rent can be shown either weekly, monthly, or annually. It may also be represented as an annual rent per square metre. If the property's total rent exceeds $75,000, then GST will apply to their monthly rental payments forcing you the landlord to collect GST and complete quarterly BAS statements for the Tax Office.

Gross rent is typically the full amount of money a tenant pays to the landlord. It includes rent plus all tenant outgoings.

Outgoings

The building's outgoings, listed in the IM pack, should include:

- Council Rates
- Water Rates
- Body Corporate Administration charges (if the shop is in a strata complex)
- Building and Liability Insurances
- Administration or Agents Fees
- Common Electricity
- Other fees that are billed separately for freehold title, in a strata shop they are included in Body Corporate costs
- Annual Fire Inspections
- Backflow Prevention Testing
- Cleaning, including grease trap for restaurants or cafés
- Rubbish Removal
- Gardening
- Repairs and Maintenance

It is unfortunately very common for the seller to omit some of these outgoing charges, thus artificially inflating the building's net rent position (Net Rent = Gross Rent – Outgoings), and hence the property value. Frequently, agents leave out the fire inspection, agent management fees, and maintenance costs, resulting in a higher net rent and a higher asking price for the shop.

The buyer needs to be diligent in checking that all of the outgoings are presented in the IM pack, ensuring your valuation is accurate. To confirm that all outgoings are in your calculations, ask for the last few years of the landlord's audited outgoings report, which they must provide to the tenants each year. If they say they don't have it, ask the tenant for a copy.

Shop Size

The IM pack will detail the size of the shop in square metres. For cafés and restaurants, they typically express the internal floor space and area for external seating. The size of the shop is used to determine the ratio of outgoings, applicable to that shop, within the strata or centre. The external space may attract a further charge from the Council or Body Corporate.

If you were leasing a shop, the rent per square metre is the critical measurement to determine the overall monthly price. As a shop buyer, it is useful to know the rent per square metre to identify if the rent is too high or low, relative to other shops in that neighbourhood. I have, at times, deprioritised a seemingly stellar shop because their rent per square metre was too high, suggesting the tenant was paying above the market and hence making the shop and its inflated rent unattractive for the longevity of the tenant or future tenants.

Lease Start Date and Lease Expiry Date

The lease expiry date, in my opinion, is the most important piece of information in the whole IM Pack. A lease term of 10 years indicates a long-tenure for sure, but, if the lease expires next month, you cannot take that to the bank. A tenant with a 5 or 10-year option does not improve the property value if they do not want to exercise the option. The idea is to buy a shop with a minimum two to three years left to run. You will find that banks get nervous when a single shop has less than a two-year term remaining, or if a group of shops in a centre has a WALE under two years.

The building or centre's WALE (Weighted Average Lease Expiry) dictates the bank's loan facility duration. Banks will limit the loan facility's term to 75% of the building's WALE, so, if we have a shop with four years left to run on the lease, the building's WALE is 4. Therefore, at 75% the banks will offer a 3-year loan facility. If you want to buy a centre with 10 shops and a WALE of 1.5 years, then they will offer a 1-year loan. Of course, this means you need to renew your loan in one year's time, incurring another set of bank loan application fees. Ouch! This is the price you pay for having a nervous banker.

If a candidate property has a tenant with just a year left on a 5-year lease, I would ask the tenant if they want to exercise their option now, or renegotiate another contract. In some cases, you may need to offer them an incentive, as previously mentioned. Waiving the annual increase is an attractive, short-term gain for a tenant, which you will recover upon the next end-of-lease market review.

Annual Rent Increases

In Chapter 4, we discussed common annual rent increases of CPI (Consumer Price Index) or fixed 3%, 4% and, in some cases, 5% increases listed in the lease, to be applied on each anniversary. The higher the number, the more valuable the property. However, a lease with a CPI annual increase should not dissuade you from pursuing the shop because the landlord always has the opportunity to market adjust the rent at the end of term.

The most common rent increase is CPI, which, in Australia, has been hovering around 1.5–2.5% over the past 10 years. When signing longer leases of 5, 7, 10 and even 15-year terms, you need to ensure the rent stays current and that the property does not become devalued compared to the market. Landlords will push for more, a fixed 3%, 4%, or even 5% annual increase are not uncommon. I personally use 3% as my standard starting point during lease negotiations with tenants. Using a fixed 3% annual increase, guarantees my rents will increase at a rate slightly better than CPI. When I come across shops with leases having 4% or 5% annual increases, this is a sign of strength in the asset and an ability to attract and keep a tenant with high annual increases.

Market Adjustments

Market adjustments are applied at the expiration of a tenant's lease and set the new rent level for the option period the tenant may be exercising. If you have a five-year lease with increases set at CPI (let's say this was 2% per year) and, over this period, the market rents in the area rose by an average of 5%, then the new rent can be adjusted up by as much as 10–15% for the commencement of the new lease. Unless the tenant specifically negotiated into the lease a cap on any market increases applied for the option period, the lease will default to this "Market Review" position.

Under a Market Review, the landlord seeks guidance from real estate agents on their current "for lease" rents for comparable, nearby tenants. With sufficient evidence, the landlord is entitled to present the market review findings and increase the tenant's rent to match the rents of other shops in the area. Of course, the tenant is not obliged to renew their lease and can relocate their business. There is a cost and lost goodwill when tenants move out, so negotiations between landlords and tenants aim to settle new lease's rent amounts rather than seeing the lease not renewed.

Building Construction

The IM pack will typically lay out important aspects about the building's construction. For example:

- Foundations: Concrete slab, brick pier
- Roof: Colourbond, tile, concrete
- Walls: Brick, concrete sheet, Weather Board, Colourbond, clad sheeting
- Size: Total land area, total building area, net lettable area
- Parking: The total number of car spaces will be defined and you should understand if the car spaces are considered part of the strata's or centre's "Common Property" or whether any of these car spaces are dedicated to your shop's specific use
- Storage: In a strata, separate storage areas may be dedicated to your specific shop in the building's garage
- The building's age: Construction date

This last point is important in determining an attractive shop, i.e. the age of the premises. I have always been amazed how many investors overlook the value from this aspect of commercial property investing. A newer building or strata offers the buyer a premium depreciation schedule, including personal tax deductions. You can expect too that modern, recently-constructed buildings have fewer maintenance concerns and have warranty coverage. Apart from the depreciation and low maintenance cost benefits, prospective tenants are attracted by modern buildings.

Be aware too that not all buildings are built the same. While some developers intend to hold the building for the long-term and hence build them to the highest standards, other developers build, looking to quickly sell for a profit. These buildings look great from the outside, but are often poorly constructed. Ironically, both buildings could return the same net rent for owners, however, the cheaply-constructed building will cost its owner more in maintenance and repairs in the long run. A good way to uncover a building's shortfalls is to ask the tenants.

Shops selling at a 7.5% return are typically older buildings with the risk of higher maintenance costs and lower depreciation benefits. In general, their appeal to prospective tenants is not as strong. I look for newer, more modern buildings every time! Be wary of a building's age and prioritise buildings that are less than 10 years old.

Depreciation

The last item to consider is highly valuable for the buyer, but rarely provided by the seller or their real estate agent. It is the building's tax depreciation schedule. A diligent agent selling a modern building, say less than 10 years old, would emphasise depreciation benefits as a selling point, as a newer building delivers the buyer greater tax benefits. If the seller does provide a depreciation schedule I would recommend having the schedule updated to capture any recent plant and equipment and to ensure construction costs were accurately valued.

If the seller or agent does not pass on a depreciation schedule, fear not, as they can be produced by a trusted quantity surveyor. I have used BMT Tax Depreciation Quantity Surveyors for the past five years. Whether your building is 5, 10 or 20 years old, BMT can estimate the construction cost and provide a tax depreciation schedule that is accepted by the Australian Tax Office, enabling you to claim the remaining years of tax benefits. So the tip for a buyer is that a well-built shop on a concrete slab with double brick walls and a terracotta tiled roof would cost a lot more to build than a brick pier, timber construction with a Colorbond roof, hence providing a larger annual depreciation deduction.

It is worth expanding on this little gem and explaining this taxation benefit. The Australian government allows the owners of income producing buildings to claim deductions related to the wear and tear of a building and the fixtures and fittings within it, this is known as depreciation. Depreciating a building can be claimed on a commercial building over a 40-year term, so long as construction commenced after the 20th of July 1982. This means you can claim a deduction for 2.5% of the property construction cost per year as a capital works deduction.

The annual depreciated value claimed reduces your personal or company taxable income and therefore the amount of tax you pay. As an example, if a commercial building cost $500,000 to construct, the government allows you to depreciate that construction cost at 2.5% per year or $12,500 per year for 40 years. This means your taxable income would be reduced by $12,500, saving you $3,750 per year in tax if you are in the 30% tax bracket, it is more if you are on a higher tax rate.

I strongly recommend talking to your accountant during due diligence about the depreciation benefits of a prospective purchase because several methods for calculating depreciation can apply. In summary, if the building depreciation information is not provided in the IM Pack, you should ask the agent for it.

Now that you know what to look for in the IM Pack and you have created a priority list of target properties, the next step and probably one of the most important things in determining the attractiveness of a property, is to talk to the tenant. I always approach the tenant first, before engaging with the real estate agent. The reason is simple, I don't want the agent instructing me that the owner has specifically asked us not to approach the tenant. I have heard many reasons, such as "the owner does not want to alarm the tenant that the building is for sale", "the owner has not told the tenant the building is on the market", or "the owner is finalising the lease and does not want the tenant knowing the building is for sale". The bottom line is that if I found the listing online, then odds are, so can the tenant. Getting a tenant's honest feedback about their business is paramount to prioritising a shop to purchase, so the last thing I want is to be held back from approaching the tenant.

I have encountered situations where the real estate agent would not release an IM Pack without the prospective buyers signing a Non-Disclosure Agreement (NDA), which prevents sharing the information or approaching tenants. Each time, I am tempted to move onto another property. If, however, it is high on your priority list, there are a few points to mention:

- This will cost you money as I advise never sign an NDA without having your lawyer review it
- Be very suspicious; there may be other reasons the owner does not want you talking to the tenant

For me, talking to the tenant before approaching the agent is preferred. The real estate agent has one mission, to sell you the property at the highest price for the owner, their client. With that in mind, agents will shower you with all of the positive attributes of the property and surrounding area. As a potential buyer, you need to be prepared with a few concerning attributes of the property and surrounding area, such as "there is little public transport nearby" or, "there seem to be a lot of other properties for lease in the area".

I will expand more on negotiating tactics in Chapter 8, but for now you need to gather as much information as possible to knock the shine off an agent's opinion of this property. The aim is to leave them thinking that you are knowledgeable and that they'll be lucky if they sell it to you, as they will struggle to find another buyer if you walk away.

The best way to approach a tenant is to walk into their shop or phone ahead and say, "I am considering buying the property. Do you mind if I ask you a few questions?" In most cases, tenants are happy to talk to you because you may become their landlord and they will want a good relationship with you.

To help with tenant discussions, I have prepared the following list of typical questions. You may not ask all of these, but they will get you thinking about important aspects of the shop and tenant's business. You should also spend time in the shop, observing customers and nearby tenancies, and drive around the local area. These core questions will determine if the business is strong, after all it will be the tenant's business success that supports your investment. You will get confidence knowing the tenant has a solid business record, is entrepreneurial, and places the right level of importance on their customers. For me, a well-presented shop is a good start.

The list of questions and follow-up questions that I typically ask, or interpret from the tenant conversation, includes:

- Do you know the building is for sale?
- Would you consider buying the building?
- How is business?
- Is your business growing?

- How many staff do you have?
- Is this your only shop or do you own others?
- Do you run and own the business yourself?
- Are you making money? Could you give me a rough estimate of the turnover of your business?
- Do you see your business staying for the long term?
- What are the busiest times of the day?
- Is the centre or shop vibrant?
- How long have you been trading here?
- Do you get on with the current owner? Have they been a good landlord?
- Does the landlord promptly fix things when required?
- Is there any outstanding maintenance that the owner needs to fix?
- Has your shop ever flooded or been closed due to flooding?
- Does the roof leak when it rains?
- Is there anything you think the landlord should do to improve the centre and draw in more customers?
- Will you be renewing your lease or exercising your option when it comes due?
- Would you consider exercising your option now?
- What was your last market rate adjustment? Did the landlord increase your rent recently?
- Are you up to date with your rent? Have you ever been in rent arrears?
- How do you get on with the neighbouring tenants?
- Does everyone in the centre get on well or is their competition in what each tenant is selling?
- Who are your competitors?
- Is there much development around the area that you know about?
- Is the centre kept tidy and well maintained?
- Have crime, vandalism, theft or undesirable people been a

problem in the centre?
- Are you concerned about anything in the centre?
- What is the demographic of your customer base?
- How do customers get to your store: walk, drive, bus, train?
- Is there enough parking? Does the car park get too busy?
- Do you advertise to promote your business?
- Does the landlord allow you to advertise and place signage on the building?
- Has the tenant mix in the centre changed much over the years?
- Has any tenant recently moved out? Do you know why they moved out?
- Who has been in the centre the longest?

I know this looks like a lot of questions, but, if you are able to get the tenant's time, you should ask as many questions as you can to get a deeper understanding and appreciation of their business, the area, and the shop you are buying.

In some cases, after a tenant discussion, you will arrive at a "No Go" decision, the property is not attractive. The tenant may indicate business is slow, the rent is uncompetitive, their losing money, and will not be renewing their lease at end of term, or worse will not make the end of term. You need to cross-check that they are not telling you a story because they want to buy the shop themselves and want to scare you off. However, if you feel that the tenant is honest, then these answers will determine where you place this property on your list of attractive target properties.

If the tenant is positive about their business, loves the centre, is making money, and is adamant they will be renewing their lease on expiry, then it is time to call the agent and have a meaningful discussion on where you see value in the building. I have another list of questions for this conversation you can use as a guide.

As is the case when you first meet or interact with someone, first impressions are important. Your first interaction with the real estate agent (acting on behalf of the seller) is important to establish your credibility and knowledge as a buyer. Having spoken with the tenant, gives you an advantage. The art of negotiation is detailed in Chapter 8, but for now you are still gathering data without tipping your hand by being too keen. The strategy of our purchase process is that we want an owner to want to sell this building more than we want to buy it. That gives us the best chance to secure the building at or above our 7.5% valuation rate of return.

In this first conversation with the agent, I indicate that "I see value at 7.5% and I am looking at this rate of return for this property". It is important to prepare a well-defined list of questions to ask the real estate agent, using your research and tenant discussion as a guide to ensure you extract as much information as possible. The following are starting points for these questions:

- How long has the property been on the market?
- Have there been any offers to purchase the shop?
- Why is the owner selling?
- Do you know of any recent sales in the area? What have other shops in the area been selling for?
- If it's an auction, will they consider selling prior, and at what value?
- Let the agent know your interest is at 7.5%, and ask if you could pursue a discussion at that level. Don't forget stamp duty and legal fees typically remove 0.3% of value, so a 7.5% offer would be a true 7.2% return.
- How long has the tenant occupied the shop?
- Are the tenants in rent arrears?
- Are there any rent abatements in place? Rent abatements are discounts offered to tenants, typically to help them out during slow periods of trade. They can indicate weakness in the asset.

- Has the owner ever needed to offer rent abatements?
- If the lease has less than 1–2 years left to run, will they consider exercising their option now?
- Has the tenant asked about buying the shop?
- Is the property part of a strata? If so, do you have the body corporate minutes? How do I get a copy?
- Do you know the age of the building?
- Will the owner provide a depreciation schedule?
- Do you manage the property for the owner and how much would you charge to manage it? (Management fees usually range from 3–5% of the net rent).
- Do you have a copy of the lease or leases and can you send them through for my review?
- Is the property in a flood zone?
- Has the property ever flooded? If it's in Queensland, did it get flooded in the 2011 floods?
- Has the area ever been affected by fire? Is it in a bushfire prone area?
- Are you aware of any council easements over the property?
- Are you aware of any major developments in the area? Your solicitor should also check this with the council; you don't want to buy a shop if a new retail centre is being built opposite.
- If there are any schools, TAFEs, hospitals, or childcare centres nearby? How much customer traffic comes from these?
- What is the main source of employment in the area? Is there an industrial site nearby?
- What is the land tax on the land the shop sits on? Often, agents will say, "The shop is not over the land holding threshold and therefore land tax is not applicable." Your response is, "I already own other property in the state, so I already pay land tax!" So, if it has been omitted, you need to ensure the owner understands that you will deduct the

applicable annual land tax from the declared net rent, and make your offer on the lower "real" net rent position.

- What's the building insured for and who is it insured with? Can you send me a copy of the insurance policy?

Remember, the agent will try to keep the conversation focused on all the positives. You need to knock the shine off this positivity to get to the true value of the property. A key tactic when talking to an agent is to be armed with a list of objections or concerns that you can raise when the agent starts getting too excited about the quality and potential growth of the property.

After visiting the property, I learn more and list out the pros and cons. Statements I use to interrogate the agent include:

- "I called in to see the shop the other day and, to be honest, the centre was very quiet. What do you think about the vibrancy of the centre?"
- "I have heard some of the tenants are not trading as well as they'd like to be, what's the owner been doing to help the tenants get more people to the centre? Do they advertise it?"
- "The property is looking a bit tired. Has the owner spent any money on upkeep recently? Is the annual strata Sinking Fund spent on building upkeep?"
- "How long has it been since the shop has been painted? It looked like it needs a paint."
- "The rent seems a little on the high side for the area. Has the owner put the rents up recently?"
- "Do you think the rent is reasonable for the area? Have you recently let any other shops nearby?"
- "My bank has already pre-approved my finances, so I'm ready to go with a normal due diligence and settlement period. Is timing important to the owner?"
- "I am looking at another property where the owners are at a 7.5% capitalisation rate of return. I like your property

better, but it is about the return for me, so I think I should move on if you can't get your owner across the line" or try,

- "The owner seems to be holding out for top dollar. My interest is at 7.5%, do you think you can get that over the line?"
- "I might just leave my offer with you at 7.5% as I have a few offers out there. As mentioned, I'm looking for a good return and there's some great properties on the market at the moment, so I'll see what unfolds. Call me if your owner is keen to move forward."
- "The tenant did not appear very inspired. I'm concerned he doesn't know how to run the business. What do you think of him?"
- "I'm concerned about the tenant mix in the centre. It's really not what I'd expect for this price."
- "I don't think the property is worth what you're asking, and you'll be a while selling it at that price. Do you have anything else in the area that's comparable?"
- "What else have you recently sold in this area? Do you remember what those sales were capitalised at?"
- "After looking at the expenses, I think your net rent position is too high. I feel the repairs and maintenance are understated."

By this time, you have demonstrated to the real estate agent that you are knowledgeable and astute. You should compare the agent's responses with the responses from the tenants, raising any inconsistencies. After these two conversations, you should have a detailed opinion of the shop and where it fits on your list of prioritised properties. Now you are in a position to make an educated decision on which property you want to buy and at what price, seeing its value relative to the strengths and weaknesses of other properties. At this point, you must back yourself and make a Go or No-Go decision.

It is not uncommon for me to make multiple offers at the same time as each negotiation moves at a different speed with different agents and sellers. This gives me choice and confidence that I can find one owner who wants to sell at or near my 7.5% valuation. It can take time to advance each property, so patience is the key. I once had a negotiation last for well over 5 months before the owner finally reached agreement on price. This demonstrates that his desire to sell became greater than his patience to wait for another buyer with a higher valuation expectation.

My aim is to inform the buyer, so that you are best placed to make the 'buy' decision without needing to refer to others. With your knowledge and research to this point, you have gained an insight that allows you to prioritise one or more shops. If you have a friend or investor whom you respect, another opinion is always welcome, but be guided by your thoughts because the decision is your journey as you follow your wealth-building strategy.

The next chapter shares different methods of negotiating the sale — preparing you with techniques that enhance your offer to agents and maximise your value and return on the investment.

Chapter 8

MAKING YOUR OFFER

In Chapter 7, we focused on doing the homework needed to prioritise and select the best retail shop for your budget. Hopefully, you have at least one shop where you like the tenant's business and the location, the lease term is long, the shop appears busy and well supported, you are happy with the potential growth of the area, and you are ready to move to the next step, buying the property. You are ready to make an offer.

I find this time of the property pursuit extremely exciting — others will find it somewhat daunting. One reason is that tied to "an offer" is a mental and contractual commitment to buy that property. Let me put your mind at ease. Delivering a written offer to an agent to buy a property is not a legal commitment to buy that property. It is merely signalling your interest to move forward with a purchase under the terms and conditions detailed in a contract of sale. Verbal and written offers may be increased and even reduced many times before the agent presents your offer to the seller, and you agree to a contract price. It could take weeks or even months after making your initial offer before you actually sign the contract of sale, making it binding.

A first offer can be as simple as an email to the agent, indicating your interest at a particular purchase price, and seeking his client's feedback and willingness to proceed to contract. How the property is taken to market determines when an offer is binding. One sale method is the auction process. This sales method is an example of when an offer can be binding. If you are a registered bidder, and you put your hand up during the auction, you are making an unconditional offer to buy that property and, in most cases, it is binding.

The step in getting to that offer is all about negotiation. If this is an area in which you are less confident, rest assured that, with the following guidance and the research detailed in previous chapters, you have the knowledge to engage the agent and owner to deliver your best offer for the preferred property. Three factors contribute to negotiating a successful offer:

1. Understanding the sale process
2. Getting the most out of the real estate agent
3. Determining the market conditions for buying

The first factor in making an offer is how the property is brought to market for sale. Different types of sale processes have different rules for the buyer. The four most common methods of sale in today's commercial property market are:

- Auctions
- Expressions Of Interest
- Fixed Price Listings
- Off-Market Sales

My personal preference is fixed price listings. I am least interested in pursuing properties that are up for auction. I will expand on my thoughts, experiences, and rules to define the boundaries and tips for each sale type.

Auctions

I find the auction process the most brutal of all on a prospective buyer. It is a one-sided affair, with advantage stacked on the seller's side. Agents prefer auctions for highly attractive locations, such as beachside or main street CBD positions, and for properties leased to national brand chains to maximise the price and their commission.

If you attend an auction to bid on a property, you need to do a lot of homework beforehand. If you are borrowing money, your bank manager needs to provide unconditional approval on the loan, this may require a property valuation costing between

$800–1,500. I would avoid bidding at an auction without your bank's unconditional approval to lend you the money. If you are using other properties as security, the bank will want to value them as well. This can take 1–2 weeks, and it is non-refundable if you are not the successful bidder at auction.

Your bank will prepare their unconditional approval and you may find a charge is applicable in the form of a loan establishment fee. The bank will need to submit a credit application to their finance department, detailing your financial position and suitability for the loan. You will need to provide personal details of your net assets and security, your savings history, your salary and monthly expenses, and the expected net income from the property you plan to purchase. The application will contain everything the bank's finance team needs to know to make a decision on lending you the money. Often, this can take up to 3 weeks, and the fees can leave you several thousand dollars out of pocket with no guarantee you'll be the successful bidder come auction day.

My next dislike for the auction process is that you need to access the 10% deposit at the conclusion of the auction. You can ask your solicitor to negotiate with the seller's solicitor prior to auction for a 5% deposit upon exchange. A 5% deposit is obviously more manageable. However, you will incur legal costs negotiating this position without a guarantee that you will be the successful bidder.

One more sting in the tail here regarding the deposit for a property bought by auction is that, if you don't have the deposit in cash and are using other properties you own as security, the bank often charges a higher interest rate for the deposit borrowings because the loan is unsecured until settlement of the new shop, which happens 4–8 weeks after the auction date.

If this is not enough to dissuade you from auctions, unfortunately, there's more pain ahead for the poor auction bidder. You need to have completed all of your due diligence before the auction date. Once the final hammer comes down at the end of the auction, and you are the last bidder, presto! You own the building. It is a binding contract, so you need to be sure that all of the checks and balances described in Chapter 7 have been completed. This means too that, prior to auction, you need to have appointed a solicitor to perform the required due diligence, giving you the confidence to purchase the property on auction day.

Due Diligence involves many areas of investigation, which are detailed in Chapter 9. However, given the auction process accelerates this sales phase for the buyer, I will highlight the important steps now. Due diligence is fundamental for you to determine critical variables regarding the property. One such variable is validating the "net rent", thus ensuring your opinion on a fair market value, based on your preferred rate of return, and based on facts your solicitor has checked.

At a high level, due diligence involves:

- Having your solicitor review the leases and any special conditions in those leases
- Reviewing the personal guarantors on the leases and ensuring those guarantors actually own real property that serves as security
- Performing council and title searches, looking for easements over the property, flood zones, restrictions, etc.
- Engaging the bank to undertake a property valuation and secure approval for financing
- Reviewing the strata minutes and any special once-off levies
- Checking with statutory authorities such as the ATO, water board, and electricity provider, and running council searches to check for outstanding taxes, rates, or payments

The benefit of undertaking these reviews and searches is your peace of mind and security. You don't want to find out after you buy the property that it floods or isn't structurally sound. Doing your due diligence prior to auction, in my opinion, is mandatory. Unfortunately, preparing a detailed, due diligence report can cost $6,000–10,000, depending on its complexity and the number of shops being purchased. This is a necessary evil to ensure that you are ready to bid at auction and enter an unconditional contract on the day. If you are unsuccessful, the time and expense are for nought —such is the brutality of an auction on the purchaser.

Auctions account for about 20% of properties for sale. The ratio is lower for more affordable properties, i.e. less than $500,000, and more common for shopping centres, service stations, child care centres, and properties over $2 million. There is nothing that excites an owner more than knowing that several buyers are willing to attend the auction and battle it out in a bidding war on auction day. If you are an unsuccessful bidder, one consolation is that any valuations for your assets will be valid for three months and can be used on your next attempt to secure a property. The auction process will provide valuable experience as you re-join the hunt to track down your next commercial property.

Expression Of Interest Sales (EOI)

I don't mind the EOI sale process because it is less punishing on a prospective buyer than an auction. Submitting an offer to purchase a property via an EOI process is not binding. That means you do not need your bank's unconditional approval prior to submitting an offer, nor do you need to have completed your due diligence.

EOI situations, however, may appear somewhat more formal because you are asked to provide a bid by a due date. This standard 1–2 page offer requires you to specify your name, purchase price, the size of deposit (usually 10%, but I always offer 5%), time required to complete due diligence, time required to complete settlement, your solicitor's details and other conditions, such as, "subject to finance approval". You submit the form, making no legal commitment to buy, only signalling your interest.

The EOI process has a closing date for offers. For me, this is the biggest downside of the EOI process. It forces you to wait up to a month and, in some cases for six weeks, to move to the next stage of negotiation. After the EOI closing date, the agent will contact you to discuss your offer and how it compared to other offers received. You can expect the agent to say, "We have other bidders who have come in near your offer. You are not the highest bidder at the moment, but you have made the short list for the round of 'best and final' offers." The other common response from agents involves them starting to squeeze you: "Thank you for your offer. You're certainly in the running, but you will need to come up a bit if you want to be the successful bidder."

After you have submitted your EOI bid, the agent begins to earn their commission. They drive potential buyers' offers up in the same way that an auctioneer does, by outlining the benefits of the property and area. In your first EOI offer, you should always leave room to slightly increase your offer, appeasing the agent and giving them ammunition to get the owner to sell. Another aspect of your offer that may increase value to the seller are your settlement conditions.

My standard settlement position is to request a 35-day settlement, with 21 days for due diligence. This is sufficient time to complete the two key due diligence activities.

- Secure unconditional approval from the bank
- Have your solicitor complete lease reviews, title searches and council investigations

If it is a shopping complex with multiple shops, I increase this time to a 45-day settlement, including 28 days for due diligence, due to the extra leases your solicitor needs to review. I have found that few bidders offer better conditions — this speed of completion represents value to the seller. Many bidders make offers dependent upon finance or the sale of another property to fund the retail purchase. This adds time and uncertainty to achieving a sale. An owner may discount or devalue a higher priced bid in preference for a lower bid with more favourable settlement conditions.

When an agent pressures me to increase my offer to "secure" the property, I hold my position, even if the agent indicates there is a higher bidder. Regularly, the owner eventually accepts my offer and awards me the sale over a higher bidder because that bid is dependent on onerous and lengthy settlement conditions. An agent once confided in me afterwards, indicating that my settlement conditions overcame the difference in price because I didn't have any dependencies on sale completion. That said, in other EOI processes, I have held my position only to be told my offer was rejected and I missed out. Even then, the agent came back to me and informed me how much I needed to increase my offer to be reconsidered! So, in many cases, EOI's turn into a Dutch auction with the agent bumping you up, until you indicate it is your final offer.

The upside of the EOI process versus an auction is that, up to this point, you have not spent any money with your bank on loan approvals or with your solicitor on due diligence. When the agent does call to inform you that your offer has been accepted, you can then engage your bank and solicitor, secure in knowing that you have an agreement with the owner on a purchase price for the property. Any money you spend from here on is not wasted and will result in a property purchase.

Fixed Price Sale Process

As a buyer, my preferred sale process is the fixed price sale. Here the owner knows what they want for the property and has it listed on the market at a specified price. These listings appear on commercial property websites with a dollar figure in the heading. The advertisements may look like these:

- Offers above $550,000
- For Sale $550,000 @ 7.0% Yield
- High-yielding property for sale: $550,000
- Offers to Purchase, Price on application

Be wary of properties that have failed to sell at auction and are now listed under a fixed priced sale campaign. As part of your due diligence, check if the property had been listed and advertised previously. If it was passed in at auction, ask the agent, "What was the highest bid?" The agent will recommend to the seller in these situations to list the property on the market at the specific price the owner wants.

A fixed price sale means that the owner does not pay for an expensive auction and marketing campaign, nor lose time on completing the EOI process. If the owner and agent believe there may be limited interest in the property, a fixed price sales campaign is an effective sale process. In my experience, many fixed price listings seek capitalisation rates in the 6–6.5% range, with owners having unrealistic views of their property's value. As mentioned, for me, 6.5% return is too expensive — 7.5% is my target.

The thing I like about the fixed price sale process is the open communicating with the owner, via the agent, and putting forward your position. You can highlight issues that reduce your offer price, for example "the outgoing administration fee is too low or omitted", "the insurance is insufficient for the building" or "land tax has been excluded". As mentioned in Chapter 7, these factors justify a lower net rent position and explain why you have attached a lower valuation to the property.

Be warned though, the fixed price sale process may become a waiting game. You need the owner to want to sell the property more than you want to buy it. Don't become impatient and pay too much, and don't be afraid to tell the agent, "I have another property I'm looking at right now and, given the owner on that one is at a 7.5% return, I'm going to focus my efforts there if you can't get your owner over the line on my offer."

Off-Market Offers

Not all properties are listed on the market or make it onto commercial property websites. Some owners are in no hurry to sell, and happily allow the agent to market the property privately with prospective clients, at an agreed price. I have, on several occasions, received a call from an agent for an off-market property, based on my previous interest in another property. Sometimes, agents locate a buyer within a day and invite an owner to start immediate negotiations. Owner's use this sale process for several reasons: they may not want to invest in an expensive advertising campaign, they may not want the tenants or neighbours knowing the building is for sale, or, in some cases, they can sell in a much faster timeframe.

From the buyer's end, the process for agreeing on a price and conditions should follow the same due diligence and interrogation as a fixed price sale, so strong negotiation remains key. In these situations, agents will remind you of the advantage you have in securing this property as it's an off-market sale. The agent will say, "It's only being offered to you", "The owner wants a quick sale, so you'll pick it up for a reasonable price", "If I took it to market it would sell for more than what's on the table now" and, "You're lucky to be getting the first crack at this property."

Do not get caught up in the "privilege" of an off-market sale. The agent is not your friend — they work for the owner and know very well the value of the shop in today's market. So, treat off-market sales the same as you treat any other sale. You must do your research and be confident in the declared outgoings, and in the tenant, believing that the rent they are paying is reasonable. Check the length of the lease. Is it secured long term? Is the net rent position realistic and true? Hold strong to your valuation at or around 7.5% rate of return.

Now you have an understanding of the different methods for property sales, each with their pros and cons. Despite the different sales methods, the questions, research and interrogation you undertake remain the same to ensure you are comfortable that the property has no issues and the price you are offering is based on your target rate of return. In every transaction, you will need to consider adjustments to your offer price, higher or lower, based on different factors about the property. For example, if it's on the beach or a popular shopping strip, you might increase your valuation. If it's in a quiet suburban neighbourhood or remote area, you might decrease your valuation.

If your valuation price for a commercial property does not match what the owner is asking, and the agent disagrees with your explanation of factors decreasing its value, do not hesitate to disengage and move on. Another opportunity lies around the corner.

The second stage of making your offer is the art of negotiating with an agent. This stage largely comes down to confidence. For me, knowing the property and area gives me confidence to engage with and challenge the agent. Armed with your perceived property value, feel free to discuss your rate of return percentage, as this is widely used by estate agents to measure value. Discussing weaknesses in a shop and resetting overstated declarations on rent and outgoings focuses the conversation with the agent on tangible, measurable factors that directly affect the property's value. Clarifying your derived net rent and the capitalisation rate at which you see value (i.e. above or below 7.5%), clearly provides the agent with your position. It's the agent's role to convince the owner to meet you, if they want a sale.

I will share tips for engaging an agent, but first you need to be clear about what motivates the real estate agent. They don't work for you, they work for the seller. Estate agents are paid a significant commission by the seller, a commission that increases if they get you to pay more. Agents will set out to earn your trust by being supportive, responsive and friendly. The agent will want you to believe they are doing everything possible to get you the best deal. They are not the enemy, but they have two objectives: sell the property and, in doing so, make the most money possible for the owner and themselves.

It is useful to become familiar with some of the comments you may hear from agents:

- "I'll push the seller to get the best deal done"
- "I really want to sell the property to you"

- "I'd love to see you get the property. It's a fantastic asset"
- "I trust you. I'd rather do a deal with you"
- "I've got other interest, but if you're ready to move now I think we can get a deal done"
- "The tenant's great. I know you'll have no trouble with them"
- "You'll be on a winner with this shop"
- "I don't see many shops of this quality come along too often"
- "The shopping precinct here is tightly held. It's a rare opportunity"
- "If you can give me a little more to take back to the owner, I think we can do a deal"
- "Your terms are good, but your price is lower than other bidders"
- "Another bidder has indicated a higher price. Can you increase your offer a little, so I can get this over the line?"

Over the years, I've heard so many of these statements. What I recommend is that you filter what the agent tells you, given their differing motivation for the sale. At this stage of the sale, you have done your research, spoken to the tenants, interrogated the IM Pack and supporting material to develop your view of the property's value. It may help if you think of the agent as merely a vessel moving between you and the owner, delivering your offer.

In Chapter 7, I guided you through the search process to identify and prioritise properties. In this chapter, I have indicated that making an offer to purchase is not a commitment to proceed with the sale. This is best demonstrated by making two or more offers at the same time for different properties. As a buyer, one of your greatest strengths in negotiating is your ability to move to another property, if the price goes beyond where you see value. I believe there is a significant upside to informing an agent, "The price your owner wants is beyond where I see value and a suitable return. For that reason, I will move on to another property I'm interested in." The agent will always come back to you and try to keep you "in the game". At this point, you may get the agent to open up about the owner's real bottom line price.

Our strategy in pursuing multiple properties is to increase the chances of securing a quality property at the right price. Making multiple offers gives you options, allowing you to disengage from unrealistic owners and pursue negotiations with realistic owners, securing you the best deal. In today's market, you should find several properties that fit your criteria in terms of quality tenants, good leases, strong area, potential for growth, etc. I've had the situation where two of my offers are accepted by owners on the same day. As the buyer, I now have the choice to negotiate the best deal and select the property I see has the most value and future upside. I then inform the agent that I have decided to pursue another property and thank them for their time.

By placing several offers on different properties, you become more patient in selecting the property at the best return — you choose on value not emotion. The influence real estate agents have is diminished when they know that you are looking at other properties and they may lose your business (and commission) if they don't convince their owners to accept your deal. I have, on occasion, had three to four offers in the market to buy, knowing that I only have sufficient equity to secure one property. All of the offers will be below the owner's expectations and, while I "dance" with the agent on outgoings and property shortcomings, I wait for a seller to become impatient and move their asking price down.

You are the one with the money and you can bet that agents will want to take it from you. If the asking price is still too high, another approach you can use is to ask the agent to "keep an eye out for a similar property closer to your 7.5% target yield". I've had them respond nervously, "Well, let's not give up on this one just yet.

Let me talk to the owner again and see if I can get him down on his asking price." At this point, stay firm and indicate, "Well, if it's not possible, just have a look at your books and let me know what else you have." As mentioned, the key in dealing with real estate agents is to never let them know you are focused on the property. You want them knowing that you are considering another property. You need to leave the agent thinking he'll lose your business if his owner continues to hold out for an unreasonable price.

I regularly come across sellers with totally unrealistic expectations on the value of their property. Remember, just because they are asking for that price doesn't mean it's worth it and doesn't mean they will sell it. I often see properties listed at capitalisation rates of 5.0–5.5% returns and can't believe real estate agents would waste their time trying to find a buyer at that rate of return. Sure enough, six months later, I see that same property on the market still for sale at a lower price and all that has been accomplished is the agent has wasted six months of their time trying to find a crazy person with too much money. This is one time I do pity real estate agents, trying to manage an unrealistic seller.

If you are among the majority of investors, like me, who are pursuing properties with borrowed money, then capital rate of return is your master. We need to challenge real estate agents to get the deal done at our asking price or find us another property at our capitalisation rate of 7.5% or higher.

In closing out these tips to negotiate with the agent, I have listed a few of my favourite responses:

- "My interest is at an 8% return, which is roughly 7.5% including stamp duty and legal fees, should I make an offer?"
- "My price is $500,000. I know it's below what your owner is expecting. Should I move on?"
- "I just don't see value at the price you're asking. Minimum

I'm looking for is a 7.5% return. I guess I should drop out?"
- "Your owners certainly want top dollar. Do you think they'd ever get that? How long do you think you'll be selling it for?"
- "Do you want to sell the property today? I'm ready to go, and my bank has pre-approved my loan. Is it worth putting my offer to your client?"
- "Bob, don't talk about next year's rent increases. I'd like to buy the property this year"
- "I was investing when interest rates hit 9%, they'll go back there again I'm sure. My interest is at an 8% return. Can you get that over the line?"
- "How long has the property been on the market? I think it will be on a while longer at that price!"
- "The most I can do is $500,000. If you can't do a deal at that price, do you have anything else on your books within that range?"
- "I see value at $500,000 and, unfortunately, above that the return is just not there. Sorry, I'm out. My offer is good. If your owners change their mind, please let me know."
- "I called into the shop and it was a bit slow. How can you justify the price?"
- "Returns of 6.5–7.0% are for brand new shops or national brand tenants. This shop isn't either and needs some repairs."
- "I think the outgoings are understated. There's no allowance for maintenance, fire inspections or administration. I'm just not getting to your net rent position."
- "It's not on the beach or the main street. How can the owner justify the asking price?"
- "I like the property, I like the tenant, I like the area, but it's too expensive. I have another property at my target rate of return. I think it's time I moved on."

All of the above statements will ensure the agent feels the real risk that you have alternatives and will move on and pursue other properties, if the owner holds his price expectation. These suggested comments are best used after you have been dealing with an agent for a few weeks and need to let them know you are ready to move on, if they can't get the owner to a more reasonable position.

Before addressing the third and last factor in making your offer, I want to introduce a different type of agent — a buyer's agent. After explaining how to choose, locate, interrogate, finance and negotiate a commercial property purchase, I would like to introduce another way: you can engage a buyer's agent. I have occasionally come across people who don't feel comfortable with the whole purchasing process and use an agent skilled in assisting the buyer. A buyer's agent helps the purchaser find the right property and then negotiates with the selling agent to secure that property. They typically operate on a commission structure, very similar to a selling agent.

Individuals new to property investing can benefit by using a buyer's agent because they will learn from their agent's experience in sourcing properties and negotiating with real estate agents to secure deals. Buyer's agents may save you time, accelerate your learning and, if their negotiation skills are superior, may save you money on the purchase price.

For me, I stay away from buyer's agents because I cannot trust their agenda is the same as mine and I do not like paying people for a job I believe I can do. I have often been called old-fashioned, but I believe it is important for an investor to learn and practise the skills detailed in this book as you build your property portfolio. My aim is to guide you in creating your strategy for building a long-term wealth engine. Your aim should be to learn as much as you can and keep building your skills as you continue to grow and expand your property portfolio. A buyer's agent, in some cases, will deny you the opportunity to develop your confidence and negotiating prowess.

The final factor in making your offer is the macro-economic situation and the location-specific view. Australia, like all other developed countries, has economic cycles that affect the buoyancy of the property market, e.g. low interest rates help stimulate higher property prices and increased sales. At the simplest level, the property market has two cycles:

1) A Seller's Market, and
2) A Buyer's Market

Over time, the Australian market has moved from one to the other. Like the tides, there are peaks and troughs. We are coming off a buoyant seller's peak, which began to slow in 2016. While the property market is slowing, it remains in the seller's favour. Let me explain the nuances of each and what that could mean in terms of your rate of return on the retail property purchase.

A Seller's Market

Since 2016, it is widely felt by economists that the stock market has been overvalued, with companies trading at high Price to Earning (PE) ratios. The populist view is that the share market will eventually suffer a downward market correction. This is prompting investors to shy away from shares and move their money into real estate.

As most indices on the stock market are trading at all-time highs, investor sentiment is negative. With the share market over-inflated, investors are looking elsewhere for secure returns. Unfortunately, the Australian residential property market isn't offering investors a safe haven either, because it's been on a strong run for the past five years. House prices are now out of reach for the average Australian. The residential property market has been fuelled by overseas capital, which many economists have blamed for creating the present bubble in values. Since 2016, however, foreign investment has been easing and residential clearance rates are starting to drop. The residential market remains elevated, with many sources predicting a downward correction.

The result of all this is that we have an overvalued share market and an overvalued residential market. Investors are looking further afield for opportunity. The search for returns has driven investors to the commercial property sector as a safe haven before a pending storm. The lure of securing a long-term tenant who can produce a steady rental cashflow is appealing. This is one reason that good quality commercial properties are currently being snapped up at unprecedented rates. We are in a period of high demand and low stock on the commercial property market — key factors that define a "sellers' market".

It's important to recognise when you are in a seller's market. Prices are just too hot and the most sensible decision is to sit on the sidelines and wait for the cycle to swing and for value to return. Even if it takes 12 months or longer, it's better to buy on value than to enter an investment that may not deliver returns for many years to come. As indicated earlier, I took my property search interstate, away from NSW and Victoria, in the pursuit of value in Queensland. My last four retail investments have been north of the Gold Coast where returns were 7.5% to 8%.

A Buyer's Market

A "buyer's market" occurs when buyers or investors are scarce. Typically, this happens when economic conditions have changed — a key indicator is an increase in interest rates. Under these conditions, buyers re-evaluate their purchase prices and attractive properties remain on the market for months without selling. Owners become increasingly frustrated and impatient to sell their properties and we see prices starting to fall.

You can't always understand the forces at work that lead to property buyers vanishing. It may be a booming stock market where potential high returns are luring investors. It could be due to banks tightening their lending criteria on investors as they are predicting an imminent downward correction. It could be talk of a softening property market, that's enough to make buyers wary. It could be government policy for reducing investor benefits and tax deductions. I am not an economist; rather, I'm a mere observer of actions that have caused reactions in the buoyancy of the commercial property market.

Another factor in the buyer's favour that is location-specific, is a projected oversupply of units with retail shops on the ground floor. This may lower prices. A buyer's market occurs in periods of low demand and high supply. I have seen several periods in my life with such conditions and I remember thinking, "If I only had some more money, I could buy some more bargains!" The astute buyer who has waited out the seller's market and has left their money in the bank is now ready to capture a great deal.

While I admit it has been many years since we have seen such buying conditions, I am confident that "what goes up must come down" and buyers will be in favour again. Keep an eye out for the following signs of a buyer's market:

1) A rise in "For Sale/Lease" signs in a particular area
2) Agents making proactive calls with the promises of great deals
3) The media reporting consistently lower auction clearance rates
4) Front-page newspaper articles of falling property prices, again led by residential prices
5) The appearance of more fixed price market campaigns versus auctions

Buying in a buyer's market means you have greater choice and owners wanting to negotiate to sell their properties. Unfortunately, for the past five years, Australia has experienced a seller's market, so, as buyers, we need to be patient, look in different locations, and keep our eyes out for value. Always be prepared to wait for the market to return to sensible conditions.

After all of your research and interrogation, you are well prepared to present your price for the target property and make a case to the agent for why the owner should consider this good value. Your time and effort will pay off. It minimises the chance of post-purchase regret and maximises the chance of post-purchase celebration.

It will not be long before you receive my favourite phone call: "Mr King, the owner has accepted your offer and settlement terms. Congratulations!" I'm sure, when the agent makes this call, you will enjoy the moment and smile, knowing that you are about to bring online another engine of wealth!

Chapter 9

DUE DILIGENCE AND SETTLEMENT

After the vendor has accepted your offer for their retail shop, you have arrived at the most important step in the sales process. This chapter details the due diligence process that allows you to move to an unconditional agreement and settlement. You will need to prepare yourself because you may identify issues that force you to withdraw from the purchase.

Let's recap the steps undertaken to get to the target property. You prioritised a few potential properties, negotiated with the agent and owner on price and agreed to proceed with the purchase of a commercial property. As indicated in Chapter 8, if the shop was secured at auction, then your due diligence and banking approvals have been completed and your solicitor has given the green light (prior to the auction), ensuring no surprises after settlement. For the remaining sale types, (Expression Of Interest, Fixed Price and Off-Market), due diligence begins now. Hopefully, you have negotiated 21 days to complete the due diligence process, but, a minimum of 14 days is typically required.

Your investment to this point is significant, in terms of your personal time and energy. You have interviewed the tenants, assessed the surrounding area and neighbouring businesses, negotiated with the real estate agent, and visited the property on numerous occasions. Your mission from here is quite simple, you must close out this transaction, lock in the deal, and ensure all of your hard work results in a great celebration.

At this point, we must navigate many obstacles to achieve settlement and a successful purchase. This chapter prepares you to respond to whatever due diligence dishes up, including:

- Engaging a trusted solicitor to protect your investment by diligently performing lease reviews and searches
- Identifying when the owner has overdue rates and other debt that must be resolved before settlement

- Responding to a bank valuation that is below your expectation, requiring more equity to secure the property
- Adjusting the timeframe, when due diligence falls well behind schedule and you need more time before going "unconditional"
- Your solicitor may find incorrect or expired leases registered on the title and these should be removed at the vendor's expense, not yours
- Recognising when service providers are engaged to maintain the building without competitive quotes, i.e. mates of the owner

If you were the successful bidder at the conclusion of an auction, you will no doubt be asked to immediately sign a contract of sale. As mentioned previously, this is why the steps in this chapter must be completed prior to bidding at an auction because the contract you enter is typically "unconditional", meaning that you own the property, once you sign for it.

For all other sale types, once the owner accepts your offer to purchase the property, the agent will pressure you to sign their contract of sale. Upon signing the contract of sale, a small deposit of 0.25% of the purchase price is paid to a trust account of the real estate agent and held until settlement. It's important to note that the 5 or 10% agreed deposit is not due until after your due diligence is complete and you have moved the contract to unconditional. This initial deposit is refundable on commercial property transactions, if you withdraw during due diligence.

Once the contract of sale has been signed, this signals the start of your due diligence period. A tip for the buyer is you can always use an extra day or two for contingency. My suggestion is to tell the agent that your solicitor needs a day to review the Contract of Sale prior to you signing it. This is a totally reasonable request. The contract may have been available prior, but your response to the agent is, "To minimise my legal costs, I decided to wait for the owner's agreement to the deal before incurring legal bills for contract reviews."

The Importance Of Your Solicitor

Once the contract is with your solicitor, my advice could not be clearer. You are paying your solicitor several thousand dollars to handle the conveyancing on this purchase. Therefore, from this point on, you take instructions from them and listen to their advice.

Your solicitor will ensure that your rights of due diligence are preserved in the contract of sale. Your ability to exit the contract without penalty is protected during the due diligence period. My advice on picking a solicitor is limited, but, ensure that your solicitor meets these standards:

- Resides in the same State as the target retail shop, i.e. if it is in Queensland, find a Queensland solicitor who knows the State-specific rules
- Understands the Retail Trading Act and has experience in Commercial property purchases, as this is a different skill set to residential conveyancing or estate law
- Is not taking leave prior to settlement. This sounds simple, but when away they will delegate to a junior lawyer and you may not get the experience needed
- Understands the multitude of title and council searches possible and ensures you perform those most significant to your target shop

I have found a solicitor who ticks all of these boxes and, after many successful shop purchases, I have exceptional confidence in him to vigorously leave no stone unturned when it comes to due diligence. My advice is simple: if you find a good lawyer, "stick with them".

Once you inform your lawyer that you have reached an agreement with the owner on a purchase price and you'd like him or her to manage the conveyancing for you, they will immediately prepare a "costs estimate" for your review and acceptance. The costs estimate is a requirement under the Conveyancing Act. It provides you an estimate of their fees to handle the conveyancing, lease reviews, searches and the legal process of transferring ownership of the property to you. We all know that lawyers are not cheap. However, you pay for quality and peace of mind. My lawyer once saved me thousands of dollars in lost rent by contractually passing risk back to the owner prior to settlement. So, securing a good lawyer, solicitor or licenced conveyancer is a critical step and should be sorted before you even start putting your offers to market. That way, you are prepared and supported when the purchasing process accelerates and you need a legal opinion.

Once you have reviewed, discussed and accepted your lawyer's cost estimate for conveyancing, the real work begins. Your lawyer reviews the "Contract of Sale" and, once satisfied with the contract and your due diligence rights, they issue their approval for you to sign the contract. This is a huge milestone as it commits the current owner — they can no longer withdraw from the sale. You are now the only person who has the right to exit from the deal, so you now control the timeline and outcome.

You sign the contract of sale and return it to the agent. Congratulations! You are in control of the sale! Your due diligence clock has started and time is now of the essence to ensure that you are satisfied with the deal and ready to move the contract to an "unconditional" state at the end of the due diligence period. For the next 2–3 weeks, you will be in frequent contact with two important people, your solicitor and your bank manager.

You instruct your solicitor to review the leases and titles for any special conditions or anomalies and to identify outstanding debts. Once you become the owner, you are responsible for the obligations of the lease, so you need to understand exactly what those obligations are.

Your solicitor prepares a due diligence report that covers all aspects of the property transaction. They ensure that the tenant is truly "on the hook" for their lease, check that rental bonds have been paid and that personal guarantees are in place, and identify outstanding issues with the building. Often, leases are in the name of a Trust or Proprietary Limited company, which can be easily drained of assets and shut down offering you, the landlord, little security. In these cases, your lawyer should check that a personal guarantee is included in the lease and that the person offering that guarantee owns an asset, such as a property or residence. You may request rental histories of existing tenant(s), arrears' reports for monthly invoicing, and any audited reports of outgoings that confirm the net rent.

A key action for your lawyer during your due diligence is completing basic council and statutory searches. These searches often take more than 10 days to complete, so getting onto this quickly is a priority, especially if you have agreed to a two-week due diligence period. Your solicitor can request numerous council searches. Some are essential while others are simply nice to have. It's important to discuss each search with your solicitor and decide if it's required. Unfortunately, you can spend lots of money, if you're not careful.

Personally, I instruct my lawyer to run only those searches he feels are essential to purchase the property. To assist your knowledge and help guide you, I believe that the absolute "must do" searches include:

Council Title Search

A title search is the most essential search your solicitor will conduct. The good news is that it's inexpensive. A title search tells you who the registered owner of the property is, allowing you to validate the person selling you the property — that they do own it, and that they have the right to sell it to you.

Another critical piece of information this search provides is any interests registered on the title. An example would be a mortgage. If the property is being used as security over a loan, then this must be removed prior to settlement. Another example may be a caveat registered on title. A creditor who provided the owner funding for capital purchases like fridges, freezers, ovens or other fit-out items, may have placed this caveat. The caveat acts like a mortgage, preventing the owner from selling the property before paying the creditor back. Therefore, any caveats registered on the title need to be removed prior to settlement.

A title search should be run during your due diligence period, so that you are know what is registered on the property's title. It should be run again on the day of settlement to ensure that any caveats or mortgages have been removed from the title.

Registered Plan Search

This search is inexpensive and provides information about the block you are buying, the land size and boundary dimensions, the lot number in the particular street, and what Registered Plan number your block is part of. It's always a good idea to ensure that you are buying the block you think you are. A plan search enables you to validate that.

Flood Search

Imagine finding out after you own the property that it's in a flood zone and was under a metre of water during the last flood. The time to discover if your property is subject to flooding is before you buy it, not after you own it.

If you find out that the property is indeed prone to flooding, my advice is to find another property and walk away. While that might be disheartening given all the work you have done to get this far, it's nothing compared to the heartache you'll feel the next time your building floods. Insurance will be difficult to get and, even if you find an insurer willing to cover the building, the premiums will be high and may exclude floods. Your tenant too will feel the pain as they typically lose weeks or months of trade and, in some cases, never open again, leaving you to find another tenant.

Water Board Search

A water board search is also essential as it highlights drainage diagrams and the presence of any easements that may run across your property. The water board may already have sewer pipes running beneath your property, or they may have an easement registered on title for future drainage plans. If your property does have sewer pipes running through it, in most cases you are unable to extend or build over these areas. Typically, if you buy an established property with an existing building on it, having drainage easements cutting across the property's outer boundaries is not an issue.

It is important, however, to go in "eyes wide open" and understand exactly what easements, if any, impact your property. Given the presence of an existing building or shop, the only downside to an easement is that they may affect the future development potential of the property.

Department of Main Roads Searches

This Department can acquire properties in their entirety or partially via changed boundary lines for the purposes of road widening or changed traffic conditions.

Understanding any road widening or acquisition intention by the council that directly affects your property is essential. In addition, it's good to know if major works are planned near your property. You'd hate to buy the property and, a few years later, discover that a major road is going in nearby. This may increase noise levels, change street access, affect available parking, and, ultimately, devalue your property. This search is inexpensive and should be on your "to do" list.

Council Fire Searches

Council requires the annual testing of all fire services in a building. This includes testing of fire reel hoses, fire extinguishers and exit lights, and checks that fire doors are compliant and not obstructed. It is mandatory for owners to submit annual fire safety compliance certificates. For obvious reasons, councils take fire safety extremely seriously and penalties for non-compliance can exceed $5,000 per day. Running a fire compliance search ensures that your building is up to code and provides you with the date of the last fire safety inspection.

Land Tax Search

If the vendor owns multiple properties and holds more land than the allowable tax-free threshold, the property may be subject to annual land tax. Land tax that is outstanding is attached to the land itself, so you may find yourself liable to pay any outstanding land tax, if it is not cleared prior to or during settlement. A land tax search costs less than $50, so I recommend it to ensure all prior land tax liabilities have been cleared, so that the Office of State Revenue doesn't come after you for it.

Building Approval and Property Search

For me, this is an important search as it tells you whether the building and any associated structures, such as carports, retaining walls, sheds etc. are approved and permitted. A building approval search details the approved structures on a property and lists any council inspections or any council Show Cause notices that may have been issued, which forced an owner to remove illegal structures. This search is a must to ensure that what you are buying is council-approved, and you are not inheriting any long-running council disputes.

Council Rates Search

This search will tell you if the current owner has been paying their quarterly rates and whether council is owed any outstanding money. My internal alarm bells go off if this search uncovers outstanding council arrears, as it suggests that the owner has been unable to collect rent and pay bills. Rates are the landlord's responsibility and their payment may have nothing to do with the tenant not paying their rent and outgoings. It may be that the owner's business interests were causing them financial hardship.

ASIC Search

If you are buying a property that is owned by a company (Pty Ltd or Trust) then this search is recommended. An ASIC company search provides you with the names of the company directors, allowing you to ensure that the correct authorised signatures execute the contract of sale.

Bankruptcy Search

If the owner is found to be on the bankruptcy register, it is unlikely that they have the authority to sell you the property as it may be the subject of legal action by the owner's creditors.

While the cost of this search is inexpensive, it may be considered overkill if there are no caveats on the title search, and should be optional and only ordered based on feedback from your solicitor.

Court Searches

Supreme, District and Federal court searches can be run on the owner if, for example, you discover from other searches that they had outstanding council rates, water rates, or land tax, or, in general, you feel that they may not be financially secure. Court searches will reveal if any legal action has commenced against the owner and what those matters relate to. For example, a bank may have commenced recovery proceedings to repossess property, if mortgage payments are outstanding. Currently, these court searches are free in all States.

I have detailed above what you can expect from the solicitor during the due diligence period. Now it's time to look at another important step in your due diligence process, dealing with your bank.

Moving your contract to unconditional at the conclusion of your due diligence period, requires one important thing: unconditional approval from your bank that they will lend you the money. You want this issued in writing.

Gaining Unconditional Bank Approval

In parallel with the legal activity of the due diligence process, you must ensure that your banker is fully aware of the settlement timeframes and have signalled their surety that the bank can achieve this deadline. The most important outcome you need from your bank manager during due diligence is their "unconditional bank approval" on your investment loan. Without securing this approval in writing from your bank prior to the end of your due diligence period, you cannot proceed with the purchase.

Prior to finding the particular shop you want to purchase, apart from communicating your intent to buy a commercial property, you cannot do much to prepare your bank manager. The bank's internal approval processes cannot begin in earnest until they know exactly what property it is you are buying, have the contract of sale, value of the building and understand the committed purchase price and associated loan you are requesting. Preparing the bank for the purchase involves you filling out lots of loan application forms and, while tedious, I recommend you do this twice. That's right. You need to deal with another bank in parallel to ensure that you can achieve the lowest interest rate by pitting both banks against each other for your business.

Finding a suitable bank sounds like a relatively simple task, but, believe me, there's a lot of science behind a bank's decision to lend you money. Therefore, it's important to track down a bank that is comfortable with you and you are comfortable with them, The best time to select a bank is when you start looking for a retail property, not when you are in due diligence. Having the luxury of time means that you can walk across the road to one of their competitors, if you feel you are not getting the best interest rate or loan terms.

The criteria I use when scrutinising a bank begins with a low interest rate, like at ING Bank. The compromise here is that ING is an online service only and has no branches or bank managers you can eyeball. Other banks may have higher rates, but provide full services, including support from a personal banker, branch offices and a fee-free ATM network. Some banks charge account-keeping fees on all savings accounts, and others do not. In fact, it became so difficult for the average customer to compare loans, the Australian government mandated each bank to publish a Comparison Interest Rate. This figure measures the total interest being charged on loans when all additional account-keeping fees are factored in, so that's a good one to look at when comparing the deals on offer.

In earlier chapters, we detailed the bank's metrics for a successful loan. The key financial metrics are: Loan to Value Ratio (LVR), Interest Cover, and WALE (weighted Average Lease Expiry). We analysed these metrics from a buyer's perspective to calculate our capacity to borrow and keep adding engines of wealth to our commercial property portfolio. During due diligence, we must analyse from the banker's perspective, which means in addition to all these calculations they will analyse one more thing — you the borrower!

The Loan to Value Ratio (LVR)

After walking up to your chosen banker and saying, "Hello, I would like to borrow $500,000 to buy a commercial property", the first metric your bank manager will look at is the Loan to Value Ratio. They want an LVR no lower than 65%. As a reminder, the LVR measures how much of your own money or equity you must contribute to purchase the property, compared with how much of the bank's money is required. When Banks weren't so nervous about the state of our economy, they lent at LVR rates of 70% on commercial property. Today, most will insist on a safer lending LVR of 65%. Again, this differs from bank to bank so, if you find one willing to lend to an LVR of 70%, they should be prioritised. This LVR allows you to build your property portfolio at a faster rate.

An LVR of 65% for a $500,000 property means the bank will lend you 65% of the property's value ($325,000), so you need to have $175,000 of your own equity in the property, plus extra money to pay the stamp duty and legal fees.

You may recall that the V in LVR stands for the property's "value". The concern here for the buyer is that the bank does not consider the Value of the property as the price you are paying for it. Oh, no! That would make things easy. Unfortunately, banks, at your expense, send one of their bank-appointed valuers to the property to appraise it and provide them a written valuation report. I have only ever once received a valuation report at the contracted purchase price. Valuers always include allowances for vacancies and, hence, typically value the property below your expectations or the true market value that the property would attract. In my experience, getting a valuation within 5% of what you think the property is worth is a good result.

So, using our $500,000 property as an example, if the bank valuation is $470,000 with an LVR of 65%, the bank will contribute $305,500 of equity. This means you will need to find $194,500 of equity, plus stamp duty and legals to complete the purchase.

For a property purchased at auction, banks generally use the auction price as the property's value, given the price was achieved through an open market valuation process.

A bank valuation is not cheap and they rarely deliver a price that is aligned with your purchase price. Furthermore, if you are using another property as security for your equity, the bank will want to value that property also. This necessary evil must be completed during due diligence and is a pre-requisite for unconditional loan approval.

The valuation process is brutal for the buyer and that pain only increases as you expand your property portfolio. This is because the bank typically requires a valuation to be no more than three months old. They will force you to re-value any property you are using as security to purchase additional properties. So, when you go to purchase your next commercial property, you need to re-value the first property you purchased, plus the second one you are about to purchase. This involves two valuation expenses. The only thing I can offer as comfort when hit with these expenses is that, when acquired, this engine of wealth will work for you for many, many years. These expenses are one-off, start-up costs.

Interest Rate Cover

Interest rate cover is usually the easiest hurdle to clear. The bank investigates your ability to service the loan. In short, they answer questions about your free cashflow and your ability to meet the loan repayments. The typical interest cover on a commercial retail loan is 1.5 times the annual interest. What this means is that you are required to have a minimum of 1.5 times the loan's annual interest in free cashflow from all of your income sources.

As an example, if you borrow $305,500 to buy a $500,000 retail shop and we assume the bank's annual comparison interest rate is 5%, you will pay $15,275 per annum in interest on an "interest only" loan. At 1.5 times cover, you must demonstrate to the bank that your free cashflow is more than $22,915.

The best thing about commercial property is that you have a safe tenant, secured by a lease and paying rent at a 7.5% positively geared return. Assuming you bought the property according to our valuation method discussed in earlier chapters, your $500,000 property would produce ($500,000 x 0.075) = $37,000 per year in net rent. With the interest costing you $15,275 per year, you are left with $22,225 per year in free cashflow. Adding this shop-generated income to income from your day job, you should be more than capable of meeting the bank's criteria on this measure, even if they apply vacancy allowances and factor in interest rate increases.

Weighted Average Lease Expiry (WALE)

If you are buying your first commercial property, consisting of a single tenancy, the Weighted Average Lease Expiry (WALE) measure is simple — it equals the term left to run on the lease. If you are targeting multiple shops or a shopping centre, the WALE is used by the banks to measure the security left in all of the properties' rent-flows. For a multi-tenancy centre, the bank tallies up all of the rent secured by each tenant's lease term. This total rent is divided by the annual gross rent of the centre to derive a figure that indicates how many years of full rent is secured by the various leases.

The WALE has a further twist when the planned shop purchase uses other retail properties you own to secure the loan. The other shops' WALE is also factored into the equation. In my experience, banks use the WALE to limit the term of the loan facility they offer you. For example, a building with a four-year WALE may attract a three-year commercial loan facility, requiring you to renew the loan facility in three years' time. I personally would love the bank to offer me a 10-year loan facility, but do you think they would ever do that? No. In fact, it is extremely rare for banks to offer a commercial loan facility longer than five years.

I can only assume banks do this because they make lots of money in fees and charges to renew these facilities on a regular basis. Secondly, it gives them the opportunity to revalue your properties. This enhances the valuations they have on record and thus reduces the risk position they report to the Reserve Bank.

You! Your Personal Banking History and Profile

I mentioned earlier the final bank criterion that we have not examined — your history. One of the first things a bank will interrogate for a new investor is your banking history. Your bank manager likes to see a steady banking history, preferably with their institution. Thus, opening up a savings account as early as possible and setting up regular deposits is a good idea. In Chapter 3, I outlined steps to get that first deposit. It is one thing to have the deposit for securing an investment property, but it's a much stronger story to demonstrate to your bank manager that you have saved that deposit through regular weekly or monthly deposits over 2–3 years.

On occasion, I meet people who have taken out loans or borrowed money on credit cards and then walked away from their responsibility to pay these debts back. They ignore the bank's attempts to contact them and operate on the premise that it won't be worth the banks while to pursue them legally. Others run up large amounts of debt on multiple credit cards and are forced to declare themselves bankrupt just to escape the mounting fees and charges they are incurring. The problem these people have is that banks keep a record of this poor borrowing behaviour and, in most cases, register the debtor's name on a "Blacklist". This is a register that instantly dismisses your chance of securing a loan from any other bank. In most cases, it takes seven years to have your credit history cleared, unless you pay back all of your outstanding debts and apply to the lending institution to remove your name.

If you have had credit cards, personal loans, or even a car loan and can show that you reliably paid them off with regular weekly or monthly repayments, it will lift your chances of winning your bank manager's support in approving a property loan.

Other personal aspects banks consider include your income and job security. In this regard, banks will rate you as less of a risk if you have held a job for several years and have established a reliable income stream with supporting group certificates. Obviously, if you present to the bank unemployed, your chances of securing a loan would be low to zero.

The banks make no secret of the fact that your job and profession matter in the risk weighting they place on you, the individual investor. Many banks even offer a slightly lower interest rate to those they deem "Professionals". I'm sure they have a detailed list of who fits into that classification, so why not ask your bank manager if they classify you as a professional. It's a pretty safe bet to assume that if you are a doctor, solicitor, stock broker or IT professional, then, in theory, you will attract a higher more secure wage than a cleaner and will be classified by the bank as a professional.

We have now discussed a few of the financial metrics your bank manager will use to measure you and the target property as a potential investment, including:

- The LVR position
- The interest cover
- The Weighted Average Lease Expiry term
- Your personal banking history, job type, and employment history

The first three of these criteria require you to have identified the retail investment you wish to buy and the agreed purchase price with the owner. For an auction, the assumption must be that you are going in to win the property. Hence, due diligence must be completed in the 2–3 weeks prior to auction. The final point is a positive banking history, this should be something you invest time in building when you decide to start saving your first deposit for a commercial property.

It is extremely educational to book appointments with a few different bank-loan managers and ask them if they would be willing to lend you money to buy an income-generating commercial property. The reward is that you start building relationships with particular lending institutions or loan officers and gain invaluable insight into your borrowing potential with different institutions.

It's important to note that different banks categorise loan risks differently. Each bank may perceive you differently. The way the bank's particular policies classify your loan risk is reflected in the interest rate they offer for the loan. Shopping around to secure offers from two or three different banks makes good sense and ensures that you get a sense for how the particular lending institution perceives you as a borrower. I mentioned earlier that I have experienced banks offering loan interest rates from 4.24–5.99% for the same property and borrower. Understanding the differences provides reassurance that you are getting the best possible deal with respect to:

- The interest rate being offered
- Comparison rate between an "interest only" loan versus a "principle and interest" loan
- The term of the loan facility
- Loan establishment charges
- Applicable account-keeping fees
- Ease of doing business, number of branches, ATMs or online presence

The banks will want to know all about you and you will want to know about them. Analysing and comparing the various offers can be time-consuming, but once you select an investment partner it is beneficial to keep using the same bank throughout your wealth-building journey. The last thing you want to do while under the time pressures of due diligence is to switch banks. Take action and select a bank before you start looking for your first investment property.

Let's return to navigating the due diligence process. Once you receive word from the real estate agent that your offer was accepted by the owner, your bank manager or lending officer should be notified immediately. You need them to drive their finance department for the next 2–3 weeks to deliver an "unconditional loan approval" letter, enabling you to proceed with the purchase.

If this is your first property, your assigned Loan Officer will immediately move to formally value the property you are purchasing. As mentioned in our earlier discussions on LVRs, the bank will request up to three quotes from a list of suppliers on their "panel of valuers" to complete a property valuation. In my experience with commercial property, I find bank-appointed valuers 30–50% more expensive than an average registered property valuer. The problem is that most banks will only accept a valuation report from one of their panel valuers, so you don't have much room to negotiate the price down. I have, on several occasions, asked them to get three more quotes and, although my bank manager was obliging, rarely does it result in a cheaper valuation quote. The bottom line is that valuing a commercial property is part of the bank's lending process, like the bank's account establishment fee, and these are costs for which you have little recourse.

Valuations, in most cases, can be requested and completed within a week, depending on the size of the property. If your target is a Hairdressing Salon with a single tenant, these valuations can be completed quicker than, say, a neighbourhood centre with 8–10 shops. The process the valuer follows remains the same, no matter if the property is worth $500,000 or $5,000,000. The valuer looks at recent sales in the area and their capitalisation rates. Using those recent sales statistics, they calculate an acceptable capitalisation rate for the area. They then apply that capitalisation rate to your building's assessed net rent position.

Unsurprisingly, the valuer will be more pessimistic than you in calculating the net rent. They will scrutinise all declared outgoings and rents and may deem it necessary to increase outgoings pertaining to insurances, maintenance costs and strata levies, based on statistical information from their "database". One thing valuers invariably do is to take a red pen to the building's declared rents. They deduct what is called a "vacancy rate", which allows for future possible vacancies that you may experience as tenancies change. At the valuer's discretion, they may take a particular dislike to the tenant type and, for example, only include 80–90% of the rent if it is a video shop, tattoo parlour or one of the tenancy types we previously discussed as undesirable.

The bottom line is that things are not in your control. You have made an offer on a property based on a particular net rent position, and you have applied a capitalisation rate to get to that valuation offer, but, until such time as the bank's valuer completes their assessment, you are, as they say, "in the hands of the gods". Until your bank manager indicates the valuation is complete and is at or near your purchase price of $500,000, you remain at risk of losing the deal and exiting the contract, according to your rights under due diligence.

Valuations below market value are not uncommon. I have received valuations so bad that the bank reduced the loan amount against the property, which forced me to go back to the vendor and inform them that, as the bank valuation was much lower than our agreed purchase price, "I will unfortunately be terminating the contract, unless you are prepared to accept a lower price." In that particular case, the seller told me to "move on" and the deal fell over. But, out of disappointment comes learning. For a while the owner did consider it. While I was disappointed, I kept in mind the golden rule of investing: Don't fall in love with a particular property. There is always a better deal around the corner. Always keep the rate of return at the front of your consideration and take on-board advice from other parties, in this case, a pessimistic bank valuer!

After receiving the valuation report, your Loan Officer prepares the loan assessment report for submission to the bank's finance department. The report details all that we have briefly discussed in this chapter: your credibility as a borrower, your banking history, the investment's LVR, interest cover and the overall perceived risk to the bank. If all goes well and you manage to jump over every hurdle, you will receive my next favourite phone call: "Mr King, your loan has been approved and we will be issuing you a letter with our unconditional approval. The loan documents for you to execute will follow."

From a financing perspective, you are free to move forward with the contract. At this stage, I forward my lawyer the bank's loan documentation for his review and let him know we have secured the bank's unconditional approval on the loan. It's now over to him to finalise the searches, complete the lease reviews, and issue his final "Due Diligence Report", recommending all is in order to move forward with the property purchase. It is always great to receive my lawyer's endorsement that he is happy with the contract of sale, that the leases are binding, and that the searches have no outstanding liabilities. I look for these assurances in writing and I often see the words throughout the report "No Liability Accepted". Regardless of these disclaimers, it is reassuring to know that my lawyer is happy for me to move the Contract of Sale to "unconditional".

Taking a step back for a moment, let's reflect on the potential situation where the solicitor's searches or the banker's approval runs late. This has happened to me a number of times. Two or three days before the end of my due diligence period, my lawyer or bank manager call to say, "I need more time to get your approvals." Your only option is to request your solicitor to seek an extension to the due diligence period. If that extension is denied, you have no choice but to exercise your right to terminate the contract.

The upside to the buyer is that most owners will grant you a few extra days of due diligence, if the reasons are fully tabled with them and they can see that a sale is likely to result. Keep in mind that, while you would be disappointed to be running late, the owner too may be faced with a whole new marketing campaign to find another buyer, and they may get less money from a previously rejected bidder. They will have incurred legal bills and be faced with a much longer wait for their money. Therefore, I've always found owners will accommodate a due diligence extension, if the reasons are explained.

Once you move the contract to unconditional, you are committed to the sale and, in reality, now own the property. It's just a matter for the lawyers to prepare for settlement and the bank to provide you with the loan documents to execute. In my experience, this process should take 2-3 weeks. At this point of the sale process, all you can do is wait for instructions from your lawyer.

During this time, your budget may be affected by unexpected charges, some may be frustrating while others are fair and reasonable. During the settlement phase, lawyers from both sides work out what utility charges have been paid on the property and what credit is due back to the seller who will no longer be responsible for the property post settlement. For example, if the water and council rates have been prepaid for the quarter or longer, then the buyer must credit these pre-paid utility charges on a pro-rata basis back to the seller from the day of settlement. Land tax is another big expense where government statutory charges of this nature are applicable and must be reimbursed to the seller by the purchaser on a pro-rata basis. This hurts more when the seller is required to pay land tax, but you, as the buyer, are not liable if you are below the allowable threshold. You cannot, however, claim a rebate from the government. You just have to wear it, knowing that the next year you will be exempt.

It's important to note that, in your initial assessment to buy the property, all of these annual outgoings were taken into account along with the annual rents that you will be receiving to determine the overall net rent position of your offer and purchase price. The annoying problem is that, while these expenses were factored in and allowed for as part of the annual operating expenses, the settlement process forces a true up calculation of outgoings, which can result in short-term cashflow exposure. In my experience, it's always a good idea to borrow an extra two months of outgoing expenses in your loan request to ensure that you have some breathing room to manage this settlement true-up process.

Finally, after the long journey of investigation, negotiation, frustration and exaltation, settlement day arrives. At this point, you are a passenger waiting for the lawyers to complete the process with the bank. Once done, you receive a call from your lawyer, "Mr King, settlement is complete and you are now the registered owner of a commercial property."

You have now secured an engine of wealth, an outstanding result worthy of celebration.

Chapter 10

OPERATIONAL CONTROL

A key decision for you during due diligence is who will manage the tenants within the purchased property? i.e. Who has day-to-day Operational Control? My strong suggestion is to manage them yourself. Learn how to stay connected with tenants while being able to optimise the outgoings. When I had less than five shops, managing the properties was possible while performing my full-time job. However, once my portfolio grew, I needed help. Luckily, I was able to engage my lovely wife as the contact for all of my tenants. She receives all tenant calls, manages trades and repairs, does the monthly invoicing, and produces the annual outgoings statements, aided by the auditor. With 51 shops, she is my full-time property manager and knows everything that is going on with our tenants and property portfolio.

Few buyers will have a partner or friend available to be your "eyes and ears" with the tenants, so, as long as you can manage the workload of the properties, it is best to do it yourself. This chapter examines what Operational Control entails and highlights how little effort is really needed to support a stable, thriving shop or centre. By outlining typical operational activities, and the service providers needed to maintain a property and the invoicing and tax requirements, I think you will realise that it is not as much of a burden as you think. Actually, when the shop is stable, you only need to produce a monthly invoice for your tenant, which is typically the same each month, and then make sure it gets paid.

Critical operational questions include:

- Should I use a property management agent?
- What are the tasks, costs and maintenance requirements for a shop or centre?
- How do I manage the monthly invoicing and annual outgoings statements?
- Does a shop within a strata building mean most maintenance is accounted for?
- How do I create a new lease and what does it contain?

The most important mindset you can develop when deciding on how to manage your commercial property is to acknowledge that you are engaging in a symbiotic relationship with the tenant. Your job in this partnership is to keep the property well maintained, in the most cost-effective way, thus ensuring the tenant's outgoings are minimised. If you achieve this, you support your tenant's business to remain profitable, so they can pay you the rent on time.

One key reason we selected commercial property as our wealth-building vehicle was due to its low maintenance characteristics. As previously mentioned, most shops are just three brick walls and a concrete floor. There's not much to go wrong, other than the glass shop front, which is the tenant's responsibility to repair and insure. So, while repairs and maintenance will be lower compared to managing a residential property, from time to time, you will experience issues with the hot water system, air conditioning, lights or maybe the plumbing, which will require attention.

Don't forget that a local plumber, electrician or gardener is just a phone call away. Even if you lived next door to your shop, you may not be onsite for repairs and maintenance, so this aspect of property management does not need an agent to manage. Sure, a local agent may have a collection of preferred tradesmen, but these are not necessarily better or cheaper.

The other key service proposed by a property agent is to pay the shop invoices, i.e. council rates, water rates, electricity, etc. I strongly recommend that you have all of these bills directed to your address, not an agent. Firstly, this visibility of the shop bills means you can manage them better and identify any issues like an unexplained increase in water usage. Secondly, if you are using an agent, you may want to change agents or stop using them altogether. Then the process of redirecting all the bills and rates notices becomes a hassle. Lastly, an agent charges a handling fee to process payments. If, at first, you want to use an agent, then I recommend signing a 12-month contract. You can always take operational control back when the shop is stable or you feel capable of managing it moving forward.

For shops that are interstate or hundreds of kilometres away and in a centre with a few tenants leaving in the next 12 months, consider engaging a temporary local agent. As new tenants will want to look at the shop, someone will need to provide prospective tenants access, and identify any issues that need addressing to let the shop, e.g. the lawn needs mowing or the shop door gets jammed.

With this background, the first operational decision for your commercial property portfolio is, "Do you have the time and energy to invest in managing the property yourself?" Real estate agent property management fees range from 2.5% to 6% of the gross rent so shopping around for the best deal is essential. On your entry level investment with gross rents around $45,000, the real estate agent fees can be $1,000 to $3,000 per year, excluding GST. Obviously, this fee will double when you bring online your second property and so on. Agent management fees can become a significant outgoing expense that, based on the tasks they perform, can instead be readily performed by you, assuming that you have approximately 1–2 hours a month to allocate per shop.

Current online banking and bill payment options allow easy access to pay all rates, to invoice tenants and to check if they have paid their rent into your account. Any issues can be managed via the phone, email or SMS, limiting the need for face to face interaction. I believe that, if you are serious about building a property portfolio, managing your first property yourself will give you invaluable skills that will serve you well throughout your investment life. Let's detail the common activities you need to manage if you take on the shop's Operational Control.

We begin with the list of outgoings that you reviewed during due diligence, either captured in the Information Memorandum or in the audited outgoings statement. Common outgoings you will need to manage are noted below. If your property is within a strata complex, all of these will be captured and paid for within the Body Corporate costs, except for the council and water rates.

Council Rates

Rates notices are no different to those you receive for a residential property, with council fees and waste removal charges. Often, these are referred to as Statutory Charges. Whatever the council sets as their rates, they are mandatory and you need to pay them.

Look out for discounts offered by some councils, if fees are paid in advance. If you have the recommended net lease, then your tenant will be happy if you secure them the discount for early payment. You typically receive rates notices quarterly, but some councils ask for bi-annual payments.

Another important piece of information noted on your council rates notice is the Valuer General's opinion of the "unimproved capital value of the land", in other words, what your property would be worth if the land was vacant. Typically, this valuation will be on your January rates notice. This valuation is important as it is the figure the tax office uses to calculate your land tax liabilities. If you disagree with the stated value, you have the option to lodge a complaint to the Valuer General within 60 days. In order to be successful, you will need to establish that their valuation is not in-line with other properties in the area.

Water Rates

Just like council rates, water rates are often bundled into the category of Statutory Charges as they are mandatory charges issued by the Water Board. Water rates generally have two components on the quarterly bill: a fixed amount for the supply of water to your property, and a metered usage component charged on the kilolitres of water consumed. Water rates are paid in arrears and I have not seen discounts offered for early payment, given the arrears nature of the billing.

Insurance

In my opinion, insurance is a "must have" item, to ensure your safety and peace of mind in owning the building. In fact, if you are borrowing money, your bank will mandate insurance be taken out. You need to insure against fire, flood, earthquake, storm damage or damage caused by a third party to protect your investment from an unforeseen event. In some cases, banks stipulate what cover needs to be in place regarding the property's replacement value and public liability, so that their loan is protected. Public Liability insurance protects you against people making claims against you if they fall or hurt themselves while on your property.

Many policies also include "Loss of Rent" cover to continue rent payments in the event the property becomes uninhabitable after a flood or storm. The individual charges for each insured component should be listed separately on your policy:

- Building Replacement Cover
- Rent Cover
- Public Liability

The tenant is responsible for paying the building cover and public liability charges, but is not expected to pay insurance for your rent cover protection.

In my experience, building insurance prices vary greatly between insurers, hence it is vital that you secure quotes from different insurers. Variations and price jumps can occur from year to year, so get alternative quotes when renewing your policy. Some insurance companies set a higher premium if your tenant uses hot oil, or if cooking is performed on the premises, while other insurers don't classify this as a greater risk. Your challenge is to get the best value for your tenant who will be paying the insurance premium in their outgoings.

If your shop is within a strata title building, then the Body Corporate will have taken out insurance cover. Check the coverage the Body Corporate has put in place because this will be for the whole building. In strata situations, it is unnecessary for you, the landlord, to get separate insurance for your strata shop.

Cleaning

Upon buying your property, a cleaner may already be servicing the shop or centre. Given these costs contribute to the tenant's outgoings, it is prudent as a new owner to gather competitive quotes from other cleaners to confirm that you are getting the best deal. As a new owner, any existing service contracts can be renegotiated. If their charges are dearer or quality is inadequate, you can select another cleaner. I have done this several times and saved my tenants a lot of money. I find that cleaning is an area where wastage or over servicing can occur and charges can be significantly reduced. I once took over a centre that was swept, mopped, toilets cleaned and bins emptied every day at considerable expense. I reduced the frequency of this cleaning to Mondays, Wednesdays and Fridays while monitoring the overall tidiness of the centre. To my delight, the centre stayed clean and my tenants reduced their outgoings.

Cleaning within the shop is the tenant's responsibility. The landlord manages any common areas, including toilets, walkways, arcades, and rubbish bins, and common ground maintenance, like picking up papers around the gardens or carparks. It is important to understand what is being cleaned, how often it's being cleaned, how long it takes to clean and how much you or the Body Corporate are being charged to clean it. If you feel that the Body Corporate could get a better deal or service, then attend the next monthly meeting and represent your tenant's interests. As an owner of a shop in the strata, you have voting rights at this meeting, so ensure that you vote for value and displace contractors charging excessive fees.

Common Area Electricity

Tenants are responsible for paying their own electricity and must enter an agreement with the electricity provider in their name. If you own a single tenanted property, electricity will not be on your list of expenses to manage. If your shop is in a strata complex, however, there will be common area lighting around walkways, carparks, gardens and shared toilet facilities that will incur electricity usage charges. In this case, your Body Corporate will need to enter a contract with an electricity provider and pay for this service, so it will be included in your quarterly strata fee. Strata fees are, of course, an outgoing expense and can be passed on to your tenant. Most electricity companies will give a discount for terms longer than a year, such as two, three or five-year agreements, so raise this at your Body Corporate meeting to get the best deal on the centre's electricity.

Fire Inspections

This is an important responsibility for any landlord. Even if the responsibility has been outsourced to the Body Corporate (if strata) or the real estate agent managing the property, you need to confirm the property complies with fire regulations. This inspection is mandatory by the council and you are subject to large fines for every day that you are late in submitting your annual fire compliance certificate.

Fire safety inspections must be conducted by a licenced fire inspection company. These inspections vary depending on the building and can be carried out quarterly, bi-annually or annually. Which particular fire inspection schedule applies, depends on what is installed in your building. Inspections could cover:

- Fire Extinguishers
- Fire Hoses
- Fire Hydrants
- Fire Doors
- Fire Exit Signs
- Evacuation Plans

The good news is that I have found these inspections are reasonably priced for the peace of mind they provide. The bottom line is you should get them done and confirm that you are compliant. I personally like to sign a Fire Inspection Services agreement with an inspection company for a 2–3 year period, so that I know they are contractually responsible to ensure my building remains compliant at all times.

Annual Back Flow Prevention Testing

For many years, you will have walked past backflow prevention valves, blissfully unaware of their purpose or why they are there. Looking like a significant piece of plumbing infrastructure, they are typically placed near the front boundary of a commercial property. They allow water to flow from the mains supply into your property while preventing anything, including contaminants, flowing back from your property into the mains supply, hence their name, "backflow prevention valves".

It is a requirement of the Water Board that your backflow prevention valve is inspected and tested annually. Specialised plumbers perform this test and typically charge around $500, issuing you a compliance certificate. Either you or the plumber must submit the certificate to the Water Board to prevent being fined for non-compliance. Again, the good news here is that most plumbers who provide this service place your details in their files and call you each year to let you know that your backflow prevention test is due again.

Like other statutory charges, this charge is mandatory. When buying a building, it's important to ensure this annual charge is listed in the building's Information Memorandum as it is an expense that I find is commonly omitted from the outgoings to inflate the net rent.

Lawns and Gardens

Early in my property investment journey, gardening was a task I took great joy in doing myself to save money. The particular property I bought as my first commercial investment was only a 5-minute drive away from my house and had a small, low maintenance garden. Unfortunately, as I expanded my portfolio the properties were interstate with gardens and lawns that were much bigger, requiring weekly maintenance.

There are plenty of gardeners and lawn-mowing service providers on the market, so finding a reasonably priced contractor is not difficult. I use locally-based retirees who are interested in a bit of additional income to supplement their pension. At times, I have found teenagers who are happy to mow the grass council strip and pick up papers for 1–2 hours a week to keep the centre tidy.

When buying a commercial property be careful if the gardens and lawns are extensive. I do own a centre with a large 500m^2 garden and, while it looks great and adds appeal to the centre, it requires constant maintenance. Gardens get pretty untidy when unattended, so keeping the woodchip up to them, the shrubs cut back, and the weeds removed is essential. There is certainly a considerable cost in maintaining properties with extensive gardens, so ensure adequate allowance has been provided in the declared outgoings.

You will not be "going in blind" on the cost of maintaining lawns and gardens because this expense will be separately listed in the Information Memorandum. It's a good idea to ask the agent for the current gardener's details during your due diligence. Before going unconditional, contact the gardener and determine how often they attend the site, how long they spend onsite each visit, and whether there are any annual once off treatments, such as wood-chipping or major tree pruning. Ask if they are prepared to continue their services at the same rate as quoted in the IM Pack for the year ahead.

Repairs and Maintenance

All properties, even brand-new ones, require some form of repair and maintenance from time to time to address general daily maintenance of the building. Note that many of these services may be classified under the building warranty if it's a new building or will be managed by the Body Corporate if it's a strata situation. Maintenance specific to your shop, even if in a strata complex, is your responsibility, for example:

- Plumbing issues: a leaking tap, blocked drains, toilets running on or the replacement of an old hot water tank
- Electrical issues: a faulty power point, blown light bulbs in the toilet, a tripping circuit breaker
- Carpentry or Handyman repairs: a loose hand railing, sticking door jam or windows, broken locks or anything unforeseen. I once had to remove a bee hive that just appeared one morning.

Many issues are once off and are typically not major expense items, however, they do occur and therefore a "Repairs and Maintenance allowance" should be factored into your outgoings. In my experience, this expense category is quite often left out of the agent's Information Memorandum. Remember, owners want to present their building's net rent as high as possible because this drives a higher sale price. Given many of these expenses are unforeseen and once off, I think owners assume a potential buyer won't notice if they are not declared. I always allow around $1,000 per year for repairs and maintenance for a single tenanted shop and $5,000 for a neighbourhood centre of 8 – 10 shops.

I have found that the key to the smooth operation of my commercial property investments and to minimising the time spent sorting out repairs is establishing a network of reliable tradespeople who live close to the shop or centre. It's as simple as keeping the preferred plumber, electrician or handyman's number in your phone. When the tenant rings and says, "The lights are out. My store is in the dark!", you can quickly call your electrician and let them sort it out.

If living in a different suburb or State to your shop, you need a collection of trusted tradespeople who will respond quickly and professionally when you ring. This may require trial and error, but the best guide to quality is to seek tenant feedback because they experience the service firsthand. After owning the shop for a while, you will develop a reliable list of trades-people who get on well with your tenants, keep you well informed of the repairs, are knowledgeable of your shops' wiring and hydraulics, and invoice you according to their quote.

Rubbish Removal

In small retail shopping centres, a 12-month waste removal contract is typical. If you buy a single shop in a strata complex, the Body Corporate or centre manager will have appointed a waste removal contractor to supply and empty the waste bins.

As mentioned earlier, participating in the Body Corporate meetings and voicing an alternative to reduce cost is valuable for all tenants. As an owner, you carry a vote. While you may represent less than 10% of the building and hence a small vote, other owners in the complex will almost always be keen to save money and will listen to any alternative quotes you have prepared.

I have found that savings can be found in waste services. Most centres will have a rubbish service and a separate recycling or cardboard service. Check the collection frequency and make sure they are not picking up half-empty bins. If this is the case, look into reducing the frequency between pickups. Be on the lookout for lazy tenants who don't bother to flatten their boxes and throw them into the bins whole, filling it up quickly. Often, a letter to all tenants reminding them that they are paying the waste bills in their outgoings helps them to understand that flattening the boxes will save them money.

There are several major waste collection contractors, such as Wanless, Cleanaway, Suez and Violia, so ensure that you gather several quotes and get the best deal while not being over-serviced.

We have covered most of the major outgoing expenses that you will come across when operating your commercial property. Many of these expenses will have been listed in the Information Memorandum, as mentioned in Chapter 9. If they are not in the Information Memorandum, the seller is no doubt trying to increase the net rent position and hence the properties valuation.

The following table summarises outgoing expenses and was extracted from a recent IM Pack for a small neighbourhood centre, consisting of 10 shops. The summary shows many of the expense items that we have covered:

Statutory Expenses

Council Rates	$ 11,180
Water Rates	$ 10,871
Sub-Total	**$ 22,051**

Non-Statutory Expenses

Insurance	$ 6,537
Fire Maintenance	$ 750
Cleaning	$ 11,400
Common Electricity	$ 5,000
Trade Waste	$ 5,500
Gardening	$ 4,800
Property Management	$ 13,000
Sub-Total	**$ 46,987**

TOTAL ANNUAL OUTGOINGS   **$ 69,038**

Notice that, in this Information Memorandum, repairs and maintenance are not included, but as discussed earlier, I would allow for them and reduce the vendor's declared net rent position.

Land tax is another expense omitted from this IM pack. While tenants are not responsible for this expense, it is a real cost for the buyer. Not for your first or even second shop purchase, but as your commercial property portfolio grows you may cross the land tax threshold and become liable to pay this. Most agents include land tax, so call them out on it if it's missing.

Creating New Lease Agreements

One other task critical to the Operational Control of your shop is creating a new lease for the tenant when required. Do not panic! Your solicitor will do all the heavy lifting. The following information can guide you when negotiating with your tenant. This situation occurs when an existing tenant's lease and options expire and they wish to enter a new lease, or when you have a vacancy and want to sign up a new tenant. It is prudent to understand the critical elements of a lease, so that you can inform your solicitor what has been agreed. Below is an example from a recent lease I renewed:

Components of a Typical Lease

Tenant	Name, Address, Email, Phone	Include company information if it is a Pty Ltd or Trust company
Guarantor	Individual's Name	Required if the lease is to be drawn up in the name of a company
Shop Size	112m² internal and 36m² external	If you do not have a survey diagram of the shop in question, then you will need one completed to register the lease
Parking	Two dedicated car spaces	A diagram of the carpark floorplan with the spaces marked is required
Lease Start Date	1 March 2018	
Lease Term	5 years	
Lease Options	2 × 5 years	This means that the first option to extend the lease is due on 1 Mar 2023
Gross Rent	$25,000 p.a.	This is a net lease, that means outgoings are invoiced separately
Outgoings	$7,389 p.a.	Estimated for the year ahead and based on the audited outgoings statement for the previous year
Net Rent	$17,611 p.a.	
Annual Net Rent Increases	3%	
Rent Free Period	3 months	Commonly offered to secure long-term tenancy commitments
Fit Out Contribution	$10,000	Landlord investment in the tenant fit-out
Signage	Position on the main sign board	
Bond	Two months Gross Rent	

The above information is negotiated between you and your tenant and, once agreed, provided to your solicitor to produce a draft lease for the tenant's review.

We have reached the end of our journey. This investment strategy leveraging Commercial property serves as a valuable wealth-building tool that has been developed and proven over 25 years of my property investment experience. I will continue to expand my strategy by adding engines of wealth to my portfolio. With each one, I learn new things and improve my knowledge to get the best result for myself and my tenants. As you embark on your investment journey, if you have a question that I have not covered, then post a note on my website: enginesofwealth.com.

Ladies and gentlemen, Start Your Engines!